Trying Times:
Alabama Photographs, 1917–1945

TRYING TIMES

Alabama Photographs, 1917–1945

Michael V. R. Thomason

THE UNIVERSITY OF ALABAMA PRESS

Copyright © 1985 by
The University of Alabama Press
University, Alabama 35486
All rights reserved
Manufactured in the United States of America

Library of Congress Cataloging in Publication Data

Thomason, Michael.
Trying Times.

Includes bibliographies and index.
1. Alabama—Description and travel—Views.
2. Alabama—History—1819–1950—Pictorial works.
3. Alabama—Economic conditions—Pictorial works.
4. Alabama—Social conditions—Pictorial works.
I. Title.
F327.T47   1985   976.1'062   84-16329
ISBN 0-8173-0254-9

This book is dedicated to my wife, Marilyn, who must sometimes wonder if Alabama history is worth all the aggravation.

Contents

Prologue   ix

Acknowledgments   xi

Introduction   1

Alabama, 1917–1945   3

Photographs   17

Annotated Bibliography of Photographic Sources   295

Suggestions for Further Reading   297

Index of Photographic Collections   299

During the 1960s and 1970s American historiography began to draw more and more from such disciplines as anthropology, journalism, sociology, archaeology, and computer science. These changes broadened historians' geographical focus and advanced their interdisciplinary techniques. Still, one of the disadvantages of this "new social history" was its surging tones of science and clinicism, its progressive exclusion of the inferential and the subjective. These key elements of the humanities, so essential to the balanced liberal arts pursuit of history, badly needed revival as American historiography entered the 1980s.

That renaissance is now occurring, and this book is on the cutting edge of it. Indeed, the use of photography to preserve and interpret history would appear to be one of the healthiest, most productive elements of the current movement. The historian, through photographs, reaches outside the "conventional" fields of history and locates new materials related to people in daily life. At the same time, this social science approach blends with an important human experience: the individual reader's immediate reaction to the humanity reflected in the photographs.

As readers enter this experience in *Trying Times,* Professor Thomason asks them through an introductory essay to remember that the years 1917 through 1945, in Alabama, involved some complex human forces. Although the central thrust of Progressive reform was over, Progressiv-

ism—"good roads," women's rights, that strange reform called Prohibition—persisted through the 1920s and helped shape Alabama's experience in the New Deal. Although idealism about making the world safe for democracy gave way to the cultural inwardness and exciting materialism of the 1920s, idealism reemerged during World War II. Moreover, during the 1920s cities grew with new industry and commerce, and they grew again in the 1940s. Yet amid the optimism over the emergence of cosmopolitan Alabama was a growing apprehension about "city life": Really, what is it? Then there was economic depression. Somehow the depression loomed as a strange result of "progress," and for the majority of Alabamians— a people whose values and even daily activities remained rooted in the Victorian nineteenth century—modernity was a double-edged sword. There also was race. Segregation and disfranchisement had been institutionalized in Alabama during the Progressive Era. But while that race system endured through the 1920s and 1930s, there were clear signs in the 1940s that proscription and lynching would not be permanent parts of the human predicament in Alabama. In short, during the years treated by this book Alabamians experienced the elements of change that reached fruition in the 1950s, 1960s, and 1970s. That the reader now can see these elements of history mirrored on individual faces—the smiles and the grimaces, the dirt and the lipstick—makes this account all the more poignant and accurate.

I witnessed the researching and writing of this volume. I saw it emerge from a scholar traveling the back roads of Alabama in an ancient Volvo station wagon rigged for photographic safari, to loose prints searching for a theme, to a synthesized scholarly comment on a wide variety of human beings and social issues. If ever the scholar followed the essential dictum of Clio—let the documents point to the pattern—this one did. So I take great personal pleasure in *Trying Times*. More important, I commend this volume to you as a fascinating chronicle—a true story—organized, annotated, and assayed with a devotion to the balanced pursuit of history as that history unfolded in Alabama.

Tennant S. McWilliams

Acknowledgments

Work on this book began in December 1980 just as *The Image of Progress: Alabama Photographs, 1872–1917* was being published. The story of Alabama's economic and social history, begun by *The Image of Progress,* is brought up to the end of World War II in this volume. Although it deals with a shorter time span, the events that occurred between 1917 and 1945 dramatically reshaped life in Alabama. It is an exciting story that photographs tell well. The book ends on V-J Day because the story of postwar readjustments, the all-important civil rights struggle, and the emerging Sun Belt phenomenon all should be examined together, apart from the prewar period. The Alabama that made national headlines in the 1950s and 1960s was a product of the period this volume covers. To understand the contemporary state we first must examine whence we came a generation or two ago. This is the job a historian is trained to do; other disciplines may claim equal or greater expertise in dealing with the contemporary scene.

Whatever their training, historians do not work alone. I owe a debt to many individuals and institutions who helped me in a wonderful variety of ways both personally and professionally. The University of South Alabama generously gave me time to work on the project with a Faculty Service and Development Award and the university's Research Committee awarded me a grant to finance the project.

Elisa Baldwin, my colleague at the university's Photographic Archives, helped print the pictures, typed very rough copy, read proof, and offered thoughtful advice throughout the project. Her encouragement and assistance saved this book on several occasions. Tamara Turk of the Photographic Archives also helped assemble copy and read proof. Sandi Mayer typed the final copy with unfailing good humor; she is outstanding in the field.

Throughout Alabama, archivists and librarians extended themselves on my behalf. The state is fortunate to have a devoted and skilled group of people looking after its records. Dr. Marvin Whiting heads the Department of Archives and Manuscripts at the Birmingham Public Library. He and his staff, especially Dr. Robert Corley and Teresa Ceravolo, were a great help. When I began the project I went to the BPL archives first. That collection of photographs may be the state's best, especially for urban life. Jo Roy, head of Photographic Services for the library, made several excellent prints that appear in this book. In Montgomery at the Alabama State Department of Archives and History, Dr. Edwin Bridges and Albert Craig, Jr., were helpful and gave me the freedom to look at that enormous, if often rather chaotic, collection. Thanks also are due Joe Caver of the Air University Office of History, Maxwell Air Force Base, for pictures of wartime activities throughout Alabama. Dan Williams cheerfully helped me to use the extensive material on black Alabama in the Washington Collection at Tuskegee Institute. Dr. Ralph Jones's staff at Auburn University Archives, especially Bill Summers, was also very cooperative. Joyce Lamont and Deborah Nygren in the William Stanley Hoole Special Collections Library of The University of Alabama Amelia Gayle Gorgas Library and Suzanne Wolfe of the university's Pictorial History Project helped me find several excellent pictures dealing with the university and with industrial life in Birmingham.

Laurie Orr Dean and her staff of the *Birmingham News* Reference Library and Jackie Dobbs of Old Birmingham Photographs also extended themselves to help me find just the right shot. The staffs of public libraries in Anniston and Huntsville and at the Hall of History Museum in Bessemer were also very understanding and accommodating, as were people at a variety of other institutions upon whom I descended with cases of camera equipment and the bland request that I be allowed to copy photographs in their collections. In some cases, after making myself at home for several hours and disrupting normal activity, none of the pictures has been used in this book. My thanks nevertheless go to the staff of Ivy Green, Helen Keller's home in Tuscumbia, and to the monks at Saint Bernard Abbey, Cullman, two victims of this peculiar injustice.

In Florence Jerry Landrum maintains an excellent collection of photographs made by his father, G. W. Landrum. Fred Meyers, chief photographer of the National Fertilizer Development Center at Muscle Shoals, has assembled a large body of negatives and prints chronicling history of the nitrate plants, Wilson Dam, and the Tennessee Valley Authority (TVA). In Huntsville H. E. Monroe generously allowed me to copy from his fine collection of photographs and to make prints from several of the negatives in his possession.

Frank Lebourg of Gadsden gave me full access to negatives and prints made by his father, Albert Lebourg, and was able to supply detailed caption information, which made the photographs even more valuable.

Professors Peyton McCrary and Lewis N. Wynne of the University of South Alabama, and Margaret Armbrester and Dr. Tennant McWilliams at The University of Alabama in Birmingham were kind enough to read the manuscript and offer their advice and suggestions. Tennant, Paige, and Lanier McWilliams welcomed me into their home on numerous occasions while I was working on this project; never has any researcher had a more welcoming home away from home. Yielding to my repeated requests, Tennant agreed to write the Prologue for this book. His contribution is needlessly flattering, but it does help to place this book in its historiographic context. He deserves my special thanks for his efforts. All the people whom I have mentioned and others besides are due my sincere thanks for their help and encouragement, but none bears any responsibility for errors of fact or interpretation in this volume.

Trying Times:
Alabama Photographs, 1917–1945

Introduction

PEOPLE usually do not need to be encouraged to look at old photographs. The pictures themselves can be fascinating, but taken out of context they are not history. Someone must take them in hand and make of them something their creators rarely dreamed they could be: the image of a time past. It is the historian's task both to find the best and most revealing photographs and to explain what they mean and how they relate to one another.

The photographs in this book come from collections in Alabama and from the Library of Congress in Washington, D.C. It is not difficult to find pictures made in Alabama between 1917 and 1945, but it is somewhat harder to find a selection that enables a modern reader to get a sense of how life was lived in that period. Many pictures are lifeless views of structures, conventionally posed groups, or studio portraits of individuals. Such pictures have value and interest in other contexts but not for this study. Some of the best pictures in this book are snapshots, photographs made by amateur photographers who had an eye for life and action. Albert Lebourg of Gadsden was an excellent example of such a photographer. His pictures often captured action at its liveliest, giving us a feeling for the people and places he knew and photographed. Unfortunately, we do not know the names of all the amateurs and professionals who made the photographs now preserved in larger collections. But wherever the photographer's name is known it is included in the caption.

This book contains only a small portion of the pictures examined. The criteria for inclusion were that a photograph must be visually interesting, historically instructive, and adequately documented. The last criterion was often the most difficult because many photographs survive in collections accompanied by little or no written information. Some of these pictures can be at least partially documented, but the frustration of unanswered questions raised by enigmatic images is often overwhelming.

Alabama archives containing the major collections have taken great strides in preserving and cataloging their photographs. However, given the perishable nature of the nitrate film in use until the mid-1930s and the indifferent processing given prints until after World War II, the images that survive are often in very poor condition. Modern prints made by copying original prints or by printing the original negatives vary widely in quality. Except for materials obtained from the Library of Congress and in a few other instances all the pictures in this book were copied by the author, using 4x5" sheet film. This procedure helped to ensure the uniformly high quality reproduction that these photographs deserve.

Despite the relatively primitive state of photographic equipment and material in use at the time, the period between 1917 and 1945 may have been photography's Golden Age. Never before or since has a wider range of talented amateurs and professionals worked in Alabama. Some are now famous names, such as Walker Evans, Arthur Rothstein, and Dorothea Lange. Other highly respected, if less widely heralded, workers include P. H. Polk of Tuskegee. Many local commercial photographers, from Mobile's Erik Overbey to Florence's G. W. Landrum, also made important contributions. Finally, the state's amateurs added revealing glimpses both of daily life and of special events.

The photographs show that the quality and character of life in Alabama varied widely from one area to the next and from one time to another. If the haunting images of poverty-stricken humanity made by Farm Security Administration photographers in the 1930s rivet our attention, we also find pictures of other Alabamians leading meaningful lives in decent surroundings. It is not simply a question of rich or poor, urban or rural, black or white. Some farmers survived the depression reasonably well, while others were in desperate straits. Some people had decent jobs when others could find no work at all. Some children went to good schools and were educated while others remained functionally illiterate.

To appreciate the wide spectrum of experience in Alabama during the period from 1917 to 1945 it is essential to search for as many different photographic points of view as possible. As good as Roy Stryker's Farm Security Administration photographers were, they concentrated on certain themes and worked only in certain parts of the state. Their image of depression-era rural life in Alabama contrasts markedly with that presented by earlier photographs from the files of the state's Cooperative Extension Service. Also, except for Birmingham, the FSA did not concern itself with the state's urban areas. As outstanding and instructive as the agency's photographs are, they do not tell the whole story of life in the state. Without other pictures they give a partial image, but one that seems complete because they are so visually powerful. Superficial examination of the photographic record can reinforce a stereotyped view of the past. A closer look at the broader photographic record of life in Alabama helps us rethink some of the stereotypes that famous photographs have fixed in our minds.

Alabama, 1917–1945

ALABAMA was wrenched into the twentieth century by world wars and depression after years of servitude to the nineteenth-century ideal of the "New South." In April 1917, when Woodrow Wilson's America entered World War I to make the world safe for democracy, most Alabamians enthusiastically supported the step. But few could have realized what sweeping changes the next generation would bring or what hard times lay ahead. By the end of another conflict, in August 1945, Alabamians could look back over two world wars and the greatest depression in history to see evidence of root-and-branch change in virtually every aspect of their lives. They had better jobs, were better educated and better housed, and had high hopes that the best was yet to come. Indeed major changes had occurred and more were coming as Alabama joined the mainstream of American life.

Alabamians, like most southerners, long had favored American military preparedness, and in 1917 they favored armed intervention on the Anglo-French side. Most of the state's 2.2 million residents were native-born Americans, and those who were not, especially those who had the misfortune to be of German extraction, found it wise to accept quietly the nation's entry in the conflict on the side of the Allies. Germans in communities such as Mobile and Cullman were in the minority when their fellow citizens began eating "Liberty Cabbage" instead of sauerkraut. Patriotic rallies, pageants, and parades were the order of the day as Alabamians, both black and white, showed their support for the nation's cause by enlisting in its armed forces, buying Liberty Bonds, or working in a wide variety of wartime volunteer and defense jobs. On all the state's college campuses young men rushed to join the army or navy or to serve in officer training programs. At Tuskegee Institute young black men signed up to protect democracy even though they would have to do it in segregated units, most of which were labor battalions rather than combat outfits. Nearly 95,000 Alabamians volunteered or were conscripted during the war and more than 6,000 were casualties of the conflict. In 1917 the state's 167th Infantry Regiment, just returned from the campaign against Pancho Villa in Mexico, was sent to Long Island to become part of the newly created Rainbow Division. Thus Alabamians were among the nation's first fighting troops to reach France. The state's soldiers fought with distinction in the battles of Château-Thierry, Saint Mihiel, and the Argonne.

Changes within Alabama took place in several important ways. The federal government established an air base, which was later called Maxwell Field, at Montgomery to train aviators. The site had been used by the Wright brothers before the war and the army continued to use the field for training purposes after 1918. Camp Sheridan, also near Montgomery, became the short-lived home of the thirty-seventh Infantry Division from Ohio. Soldiers from the Midwest flooded the capital. The 20,000-man camp, one-third the size of the city itself, had a social and economic impact on the "Cradle of the Confederacy" that would be hard to overestimate. Thousands of soldiers from other parts of the nation also were stationed at Anniston's Camp McClellan.

War-related industries brought further social and economic change to Alabama. The people of the state's mineral region saw skyrocketing wartime orders for coal, steel, and pig iron. The Tennessee Coal and Iron Company (TCI) built new facilities at Fairfield to make steel for ships and a shipyard to build them at Chickasaw near Mobile. Iron and steel mills worked at full capacity. With men away in the service, and with business booming, unemployment ceased to be a problem, at least among urban whites. Women moved into some jobs previously reserved for men, while all over Alabama females left home to serve as secretaries, drivers, telephone operators, and nurses. Despite segregation laws many blacks also found work at army camps and on federal projects including those at Muscle Shoals on the Tennessee River.

The National Defense Act of 1916 had authorized the construction of a hydroelectric dam and nitrate plants at Muscle Shoals. The purpose was to produce an adequate supply of nitrate for explosives using a process that required a large amount of electricity. The 134-foot fall of the Tennessee River in the region around Muscle Shoals, if harnessed by a hydroelectric dam, would provide more than adequate electricity. Supporters of the project argued that the nitrate also could be used in peacetime to make

fertilizer to help the region's sagging agricultural production. Initially Congress authorized $20 million for the project, but before the Harding administration ended work on the dam, named in honor of Woodrow Wilson, more than $120 million would be spent. The chemical plants were completed too late to provide nitrate for munitions and Wilson Dam was not finished when its construction was halted. However, both projects provided large construction payrolls for a chronically depressed region of the state. They also raised hopes of peacetime economic revival fueled by abundant cheap electricity and fertilizer. Unfortunately, these hopes would not be realized until after the Tennessee Valley Authority was established in 1933.

During the war, the state's port city, Mobile, enjoyed its best times since antebellum days. Orders for ships meant new jobs and even new shipyards. Anticipating the demand, United States Steel's TCI subsidiary had begun construction of its Chickasaw shipyard in 1914. Two years later the Alabama Dry Dock and Shipbuilding Company was formed by the merger of several older Mobile yards. The Port City's shipbuilders would experiment with a variety of ship designs but the war's end halted such innovations. Several of the ships begun during the conflict were not even launched until after its conclusion.

The impact of defense industries and military establishments on life in Alabama came to an abrupt halt with the signing of the armistice on November 11, 1918. Bases were closed, contracts were cancelled, and payrolls were slashed. The war's end also meant an end to the slaughter and a return home for Alabama's servicemen. Celebrations were held across the state as news of the armistice reached Alabama. Mobile's lasted all day as 10,000 people jammed into the city's center. It was not until the following spring, after a devastating flu epidemic had ravaged Europe and the United States in the winter of 1918–19, that the Alabama's 167th Regiment (now known as the "Fighting Fourth") came home. Returning soldiers were accorded a hero's welcome in Mobile, Birmingham, and Montgomery as large crowds turned out to cheer their arrival. But they would find farm prices depressed and jobs hard to come by in the cities, as Alabama wrestled with a postwar depression.

In many ways World War I's impact on Alabama offered a preview of what would occur during the more protracted Second World War. A large percentage of young men entered the service; military training facilities were established, bringing thousands of servicemen from other parts of the country into the state; defense-related industry boomed; and women found new job opportunities. Alabamians of all ages, black and white, demonstrated their patriotism through national service and by buying war bonds. In both wars impoverished farmers left the land searching for decent jobs in the state's war industries. In World War I black Alabamians were barred by segregation laws from most wartime economic opportunities. The situation improved somewhat in World War II, though segregation continued.

Not all the issues facing Alabamians after World War I were economic. In 1920, nationwide Prohibition was approved and women gained the right to vote. Alabama long had favored the former and opposed the latter, despite strenuous efforts for many years by the state's suffragists. Granting women the right to vote did not bring about a revolution or the collapse of domestic institutions as some had feared, nor did it noticeably raise the tenor of political debate. Prohibition, dubbed the "noble experiment," made lawbreakers out of a generation of Alabamians, but it did give a young attorney, Hugo Black, a chance to make a name for himself by prosecuting bootleggers in Mobile.

As part of a national protest over postwar wage reductions in the bituminous coal industry, labor unrest flared in the Birmingham area in the winter of 1919–20 when the United Mine Workers went on strike. Newly elected Governor Thomas Kilby sent in the state militia to break up the tent cities where the miners were living, and the strike ended. Strikers were blackballed by the industry and the union was destroyed. The UMW did not recover from this defeat until after the National Industrial Recovery Act of 1934. Kilby's actions in the 1919–20 strike were entirely in keeping with his probusiness orientation. But he also set out to reform and "improve" Alabama by approaching its problems in a "businesslike" way. He was a Progressive who believed in orderly review and reform but feared and opposed anything smacking of "revolution." Kilby spearheaded reform of the convict leasing system and the construction of a modern state prison that subsequently was named for him. He saw the establishment of a state board of education designed to set and enforce uniform minimum school standards throughout Alabama. He supported the state's first workman's compensation law and favored the elimination of child labor.

The progressivism of Kilby and his allies throughout the state was rooted in the conviction that whatever problems Alabama faced could be solved only if business leaders were satisfied with the present and optimistic about the future. Progressives in Alabama believed that the government had a responsibility to enhance the environment in which business operated not only by keeping labor cheap and taxes low but also by undertaking certain public works. One of Alabama's great needs after World War I was a modern transportation system, specifically all-weather roads throughout the state and improved port facilities at Mobile and Birmingham. In 1916 Alabama Senator John Bankhead, Sr., had sponsored the Good Roads Act, which authorized the federal government to match, dollar for dollar, state expenditures on federal highways. With Kilby's support the legislature authorized the first road construction bond issue for $25 million to take advantage of these federal funds. The state undertook road construction in every Alabama county thereafter.

Mobile's antiquated port facilities long had retarded the state's economic development. In 1915 the federal government had completed a series of locks and dams on the Black Warrior River, enabling barge traffic to go from Birmingham to Mobile. The absence of an adequate port facility at Birmingham, however, limited the volume of traffic. World War I had seen a growth of all types of shipping in and out of Mobile and between Mobile and Birmingham, but Mobile could not handle the tonnage efficiently. In 1920 Birmingham's port facility on the Black Warrior River was completed and barge traffic increased rapidly. The port of Mobile was neither large nor modern enough to meet the subsequent demand. Since 1915 Mobilians had urged the state to construct a modern docks complex. The world war interrupted progress, but finally in 1922, with Governor Kilby's backing and support from business leaders across the state, Mobile's long battle was successful. Voters approved a necessary amendment to the constitution. The legislature established a state docks commission, which authorized a $10 million bond issue, and

construction began on a 540-acre site north of Mobile. When completed and dedicated in June 1928, Alabama had the most modern shipping facility in the nation.

By the end of Kilby's term in 1923, signs of a return of prosperity could be seen in many of Alabama's towns and cities. Business was not booming, but there seemed clear cause for optimism. However, prosperity was far from being evenly distributed. Wages remained low for workers in the state's urban areas while much of rural Alabama, including the Tennessee Valley, remained in a chronic state of depression. Because most Alabamians lived in rural areas or in small towns, the condition of the state's farm economy was crucially important. Although one of the goals of the Good Roads Movement had been to improve farm-to-market roads to aid the state's farmers, rural Alabama got little else from the urban-oriented Progressive program.

Alabama's farmers in the 1920s suffered from both short- and long-term disabilities. In the short term, they had faced falling prices for their principal crop after 1914 when the war interrupted cotton sales to Europe. Prices for all agricultural produce collapsed abruptly after the armistice when the army stopped buying. The second short-term disability Alabama's cotton farmers faced was the boll weevil, a pest from Mexico that repeatedly destroyed crops after 1914, obliging diversification into peanuts, soybeans, corn, and livestock. As a symbol of their release from their thralldom to King Cotton, farmers in the Wiregrass region erected a statue to the boll weevil in Enterprise in 1919. But many farmers were not able to give up growing cotton because of their status as tenant farmers or sharecroppers.

Sharecropping and tenancy were long-standing disabilities

that grew out of the period following the Civil War. When slavery was ended, planters had land but no laborers and black laborers had no land on which to work. Eventually many of these former slaves were allowed to farm land in exchange for a share of the crop they grew. White farmers who owned land often had to mortgage their future crops in order to get food and necessities from year to year. They often lost their land, becoming tenants on farms they once had owned. The merchants who "furnished" supplies in exchange for a share of the anticipated crop, or the planters who provided land and other necessities on the same terms, wanted cotton grown because the crop was more easily stored, transported, and sold than perishable foodstuffs. As cotton production in Alabama increased, despite the attacks of pests such as the boll weevil or the gradual devastation of the land caused by intensive cotton cultivation, prices fell. Poor farmers worked harder, planted more cotton, and received less for their trouble at harvest time. During World War I thousands of disgruntled farmers left the Black Belt looking for work in the cities or leaving the state for the North and West. Some returned when defense jobs ended, but most did not. There was never incentive for innovation; in areas where sharecropping was most prevalent crop yields were the lowest.

The Alabama Polytechnic Institute (later Auburn University, and hereafter so cited), Tuskegee Institute, and the state's county agents worked throughout the 1920s demonstrating scientific farming principles, crop alternatives to cotton, and improved animal husbandry. Such programs had little impact among King Cotton's tenants as they tried to beat the system, hoping for a combination of a good year and high prices for their crop. As the decade progressed, erosion claimed more and more worn-out land, until by 1930 the state had lost nearly one million acres of arable land.

Educational opportunities in Alabama's rural counties were generally much poorer than in its cities. Despite efforts at reform before World War I, rural counties spent far less per pupil than their urban counterparts. Statewide per pupil expenditures for black schools were a minor fraction of those for whites. In 1930 black teachers in Alabama were paid less than one-third the salary of their white counterparts. The predictable result was an illiteracy rate among black youngsters that was three times higher than that among whites. At least one in four of school-aged black children was unable to read and write, as opposed to one in twelve among whites. Blacks were far more likely to attend one-room schoolhouses than were whites, and blacks often were denied opportunity for any education beyond the primary level. In urban counties where black children could attend high schools, they usually went to industrial or training schools emphasizing vocational education.

Not all Alabamians saw the need for formal education. The parents of rural black and white children often took them out of school to help with farming activities, so that they received even less education than they might have. Nevertheless, progress was made in the 1920s. As roads were paved many small rural schools were consolidated and modern facilities were built. Under the administration of Progressive Governor Bibb Graves (1927–31) $17 million was appropriated for education and a minimum program was developed for all school systems in the state. Graves also succeeded in getting the legislature to pass an amendment to the state constitution that would have provided $20 million for school construction. But this provision was too much for those who feared additional taxes. Alabama's voters rejected the amendment. Despite the setback, Graves had managed to make progress toward raising the state's appallingly low educational standards. However, the collapse of Alabama's economy, which began even before the crash on Wall Street, managed to undo much of his work as state tax revenues plummeted.

The governor's commitment to education was matched by his determination to continue to expand the intensive road-building program begun in the Kilby administration. Roads and bridges were constructed throughout Alabama, financed by a $25 million bond issue and a gasoline tax of two cents per gallon. Graves and his supporters pointed to the economic benefits of a modern road system and the increasing importance of the automobile in moving goods and people. During Graves's first year in office one of the most impressive road-building projects, the Cochrane Bridge causeway across Mobile Bay, was completed, financed by an independent authority's bond issue rather than by state money. The causeway made possible an expansion of the region dominated by businesses in Mobile, facilitated east–west travel from Jacksonville, Florida, to San Diego, California, and made possible tourism as a significant element in Mobile's economy. With the causeway's completion the Port City saw the inauguration of the Azalea Trail, the annual fishing rodeo off Dauphin Island, and in 1932 the opening of Bellingrath Gardens south of the city. All three brought tourists to Mobile and delighted residents as well. These were the kinds of results anticipated by supporters of other road-building projects in Alabama in the 1920s. Graves had helped dedicate the Cochrane Bridge in 1927; a decade later during his second term as governor he would lift the toll on this and all other roads and bridges around the state.

Building on Kilby's prison reforms, Graves eliminated convict leasing in 1927, an evil the state had practiced for almost half a century. State and county prisoners had been leased to corporations, especially coal-mining companies, at very low rates. Large numbers labored in the mines around Birmingham, and over the years the treatment of prisoners had shocked many Alabamians. Graves's move to end the practice was especially popular with his supporters in organized labor. Union leaders always had felt that the convict leasing system, by providing cheap labor, kept all wages low and discouraged free men from organizing unions. Convicts continued to work after 1927 but on state and county farms, road gangs, and in prison industries.

Although Graves was a Progressive, believing that the government can and should help the average citizen and encourage business growth, he also depended upon the political support of the Ku Klux Klan. Indeed, he was an official in the Montgomery Klavern. In the mid-1920s the Klan openly flaunted its political power throughout Alabama. Graves was by no means the only important official elected with strong Klan support. Many city commissioners and a variety of county and state officials owed allegiance to the hooded order. Even Hugo Black, whose subsequent career in the United States Senate and on the United States Supreme Court marked him as a stalwart defender of individual rights, originally was elected to the Senate in 1926 with Klan backing. He had joined the Robert E. Lee Klavern of Birmingham in order to further his political ambitions. He and others knew that election to public office was virtually impossible without Klan support.

The Klan began to fade from the scene in the late

1920s after courageous attacks upon it by Grover Hall, editor of the *Montgomery Advertiser,* and by others across the state. For most of the decade the Klan had exercised awesome political power. In addition to political activity, it engaged in intimidation, floggings, and other acts of mayhem. Indeed, its activities were not directed primarily against the state's black people, who were already effectively excluded from political, economic, and social influence by the barriers of segregation. In defense of its brand of white Protestantism, the hooded order sought to extend that exclusion to ethnic and religious groups that lay outside the mainstream of rural Alabama's experience. Thus, "wets," Jews, Catholics, and foreigners all were their targets. Many of the Klansmen were rural folk who had come to the city looking for work. In a threatening and unfamiliar environment, the Klan offered them something in which to believe and belong, perhaps overcoming their sense of powerlessness. It also gave them convenient scapegoats for their troubles. Even in Birmingham Klan membership collapsed at the end of the decade, not because ethnic and racial animosities had eased, but because the Klan leadership was crooked, had duped its own followers, and was denounced by some of the civic and religious leaders who once had supported it. Although animosity toward Jews, foreigners, and blacks resurfaced in the 1930s in reaction to the famous Scottsboro rape case, it lacked the organization and hooded anonymity that had made the Klan such an alarmingly potent social and political force in the 1920s.

Although Alabama's total population grew by only 10 percent in the 1920s, the decade saw dramatic growth in the population of Birmingham, which grew by a third. The Magic City's economy could not absorb these newcomers, especially as the pace of its economic activity slowed after 1927. Birmingham's iron and steel had been effectively overpriced as a result of the "Pittsburgh Plus" formula, used to figure prices for United States Steel's products. Iron and steel were priced the same as Pittsburgh's, plus the cost of freight from the Pennsylvania city and the actual cost of shipping from Birmingham. When orders lagged in the late 1920s, U.S. Steel kept its Pittsburgh mills working by putting the Birmingham facilities on short time or by closing them entirely.

As students of the Great Depression have noted, a principal cause of the calamity was the imbalance between productivity and buying power. Working for low wages or depressed agricultural prices, Alabamians were a poor market for the goods they and other Americans produced. Add to this disparity between production and consumption a freewheeling system of credit for investors and a federal government unwilling to provide needed regulation, and it is little wonder that the national economy stumbled toward collapse. Also, international economic activity had not recovered from the effects of the world war, reparations, inflation, and European political instability. Thus Alabama was swept up in the maelstrom that struck the whole world, beginning with European and American bank failures and the stock market crash in October 1929.

Early in the depression Birmingham earned the dubious distinction of being the hardest-hit city in the country, and the state's farmers saw cotton prices fall to five cents a pound. Government debt in Alabama climbed as tax collections lagged and the expenses of early relief measures and Graves's road and school policies mounted. Retrenchment became the order of the day at all levels of government.

President Herbert Hoover set the pace by refusing to use federal funds in direct relief measures. By the eve of the presidental elections in 1932, one out of four workers in Birmingham was out of a job. Statewide retail sales were half their 1928 level, and sales of durable goods had fallen by 90 percent. Men and women living in hobo jungles on the outskirts of Mobile and most other metropolitan centers depended upon handouts and help from overextended private charities. Much of Alabama's arable land lay eroded and useless and the remainder was exhausted from overcropping. More than 60 percent of Alabama's farmers were tenants, most of them working land they had occupied for less than a year. Besides moving from farm to farm, the rural poor were leaving counties in the Black Belt by the thousands, deserting its worn-out land and making ghost towns of small communities in the region. In the Tennessee Valley hard times seemed even worse as the idle Wilson Dam served as a constant reminder of what might have been.

In the early 1920s, while debate raged in Congress about the future of the Muscle Shoals nitrate plants and dam, Henry Ford offered to buy the facilities for pennies on the dollar and to complete them. High hopes for Ford's proposed Seventy-Five Mile City, to be built around the power-generating capacity of the dam, collapsed when Ford subsequently withdrew his offer. For the remainder of the decade no alternative won the approval of the Republican-controlled White House, so the plants and dam were unused and the region remained chronically depressed.

In the depths of the greatest depression in American history, the voters in Alabama joined the rest of the nation in electing Franklin Delano Roosevelt. Although a native New Yorker, Roosevelt had spent many years at Warm Springs, Georgia, and understood the South's desperate economic plight. He traveled through Alabama to the Tennessee Valley shortly after his election and before he was inaugurated as president. A few months later, on May 18, 1933, he returned in triumph to Muscle Shoals to sign the Morris-Hill bill establishing the Tennessee Valley Authority. TVA would transform the valley, bringing industrial development to the region by providing abundant hydroelectric power. It also would use the nitrate plants to conduct long-term research projects and to produce cheap fertilizer that would help to revitalize agriculture there and throughout the state.

Besides establishing the TVA during his whirlwind "Hundred Days," Roosevelt took steps to shore up the state's crumbling banking industry and to pump federal money into direct, work-relief operations that were already in place. In the months that followed, Alabamians became familiar with an alphabet soup of federal agencies that sought to ameliorate the hardships of the depression. Many of the New Deal programs were designed to aid farmers. The Agriculture Adjustment Act put nearly $36 million into the pockets of farmers in the state between 1933 and 1936 plus $5 million more in price-support payments divided between landlord and tenant. The Farm Security Administration loaned $8 million to more than 24,000 farm families to use for rent, taxes, and food or to purchase supplies and equipment. The Civilian Conservation Corps undertook erosion-control projects in various parts of Alabama. Direct agreements between various federal agencies and individual farmers to undertake erosion-control and reforestation measures were in effect for 400,000 acres in the state by 1940. One unfortunate legacy of these projects throughout the South is kudzu, a vine planted to control erosion. The degree of its successful adaptation to the climate and soil of the region was unexpected. The Rural Electrification Administration brought electricity to many of the state's farms for the first time. Federal agencies also worked with Auburn's network of experimental stations and county agents to supply information on scientific farming, farm management, and nutrition.

Despite all the work of federal and state agencies, the agricultural system, still tied to tenancy and cotton, continued to decay. Some federal programs designed to help both tenant and landlord by paying for reduced agricultural production simply enabled landlords to evict tenants and turn to raising livestock. Erosion-control measures were dwarfed by the growing problem. By the mid-1930s nearly four million acres of farmland were either destroyed or threatened with destruction. Farmland that had been worth an average of $28.00 an acre as recently as 1928 sold for $19.00 in 1935—when buyers could be found.

Hard times also tended to exacerbate racial tensions. Whites feared black competition for the few available jobs and lived with a more nebulous terror of widespread racial violence. Against this background nine young black men were pulled off a freight train at Scottsboro in 1931 and were charged with raping two white girls who also were hoboing on the train. Despite the absence of reliable witnesses or medical corroboration that an attack even had taken place, the nine "boys" were convicted and sentenced to die. The case against them was so outrageously weak and racially motivated that soon a storm of national and international protest overwhelmed the state. The National Association for the Advancement of Colored People joined with the Communist party's Legal Defense Fund to secure an appeal. In 1932, the result of that appeal was a United States Supreme Court order for a new trial on the grounds that the defendants had not had adequate legal counsel. At a second trial, despite the recanting of the whole story by one of the girls, the boys were convicted again. Another appeal eventually overturned that verdict with the precedent-setting decision that, inasmuch as no blacks were eligible for jury duty, the defendants were denied the equal protection of the laws guaranteed by the Fourteenth Amendment. In 1937, a third trial saw five defendants convicted, four set free. Bibb Graves eventually commuted the death sentences imposed by the court. As the years passed, five gained their freedom, one by escaping, but the last man was not released until 1950. In the 1930s, some Alabamians had questioned the justice of the Scottsboro proceedings, but for most the race of the accused and the involvement of the Communist party and the NAACP on their behalf were enough to establish guilt.

Industrial strife also rocked Alabama during the decade as many workers in the state's mines and mills struggled to organize unions. Leading the fight was John L. Lewis and the Congress of Industrial Organizations. By the end of 1934 Lewis had seen his United Mine Workers establish more than ninety locals with 23,000 members in the state. In 1937 the CIO finally won a contract with the Tennessee Coal and Iron Company. Union membership in Birmingham soared from 2,000 in 1930 to 50,000 in 1934 with the CIO reaping most of the gains. The National Industrial Recovery Act, which was passed in 1934 to protect workers' rights to organize a union, contributed to this dramatic rise in membership. Not all workers or all mines and mills were unionized, nor was the process without violence. The DeBardeleben mines remained non-unionized, and violent conflicts occurred between union and anti-union forces. By the end of the decade coal, iron, steel, and maritime workers were organized although textile and farm workers were not. Federal legislation from

NIRA to the Fair Labor Standards Act of 1938 helped to ensure better wages and a shorter work week. The FLSA also brought an end to the lingering evil of child labor.

Leading the fight for many of FDR's measures in Congress were Alabama's congressmen and senators. George Huddleston, Henry Steagall, Hugo Black, Lister Hill, and William Bankhead all were staunch supporters of the New Deal and the authors of many of its key measures. Alabamians also filled a variety of administrative roles in the federal government. Edward O'Neal III, president of the American Farm Bureau, was Roosevelt's chief adviser on farm issues. Aubrey Williams headed the National Youth Administration, and Thad Holt directed a variety of relief agencies, including the Alabama Works Progress Administration (WPA).

The WPA became the symbol of the New Deal for many Alabamians. It undertook relief projects in every county of the state. WPA workers cleared streams; built public buildings, airports, roads, and bridges; conducted historical research; and organized artistic and theatrical ventures. The WPA created jobs, paid a living wage, and gave workers a chance once again to feel that they were productive members of society. The prototype of the WPA was the Alabama Relief Administration, which had been established shortly before Roosevelt was sworn into office. The ARA lasted for two years, directing work-relief projects financed with federal funds through the Civil Works Administration. It employed 129,000 people and spent $15 million by April 1, 1934, when the CWA was phased out and the WPA took over public works programs. The WPA handled several large-scale tasks, including relocating Vulcan's statue in a park on Red Mountain in Birmingham. But its hallmark was its flexibility in dealing with a variety of projects, most of them modest in scale. The Public Works Administration was intended to oversee larger jobs by independent contractors. For example, the PWA supervised the construction of the Bankhead Tunnel under the Mobile River, a project that was completed in 1941. By that year, most of FDR's New Deal agencies were being phased out as the United States prepared for war.

Signs of industrial recovery could be seen in Alabama as early as 1934 when TCI received the first of a series of large orders from railroads for steel rails, but sustained recovery came only as war clouds began to gather in the late thirties. For example, the port of Mobile was busy shipping scrap iron to "the Japs, the Germans and whoever else would buy" when North Carolina newspaper editor Jonathan Daniels visited the city in 1937. In the same year the Aluminum Company of America began construction of a major plant in Mobile. It was followed in short order by National Gypsum, American Cyanamid, and Pan-American Shell Corporation. By 1940 the U.S. Army Air Corps had begun building Brookley Field while thousands of workers were being hired by the Alabama Dry Dock and Shipbuilding Company, and by U.S. Steel's Gulf Shipyards. The shipbuilding and repair industry had begun its spectacular wartime boom nearly two years before the United States entered the war.

Across the state other cities and towns shared Mobile's experience in the last years of the depression decade. In 1940 the air corps took over Montgomery's municipal airport and established what became Gunter Field. Twelve thousand pilots received their basic training there during the war. In the same year Maxwell Field operations were expanded dramatically as it became the training center for air corps bomber crews. During the war more than 2,600 B-24 crews and 728 B-29 crews would fly out of Maxwell. A total of 100,000 cadets were trained at the facility by war's end. Craig Field in Selma and Moton Field in Tuskegee also were established by the army air corps. Both were training bases for fliers, but Moton Field was notable as the site of the first facility for black pilots. It was established in 1941 after the air corps yielded to intensive NAACP pressure to allow black Americans to train and serve as pilots. Fort McClellan, near Anniston, was reactivated in 1940 and, in the Wiregrass region, Camp Rucker was established for infantry training. Huntsville became home to a multimillion-dollar army chemical warfare plant and to the smaller Redstone Ordnance plant that produced artillery shells and other weapons. These two facilities brought 20,000 new jobs to Huntsville during the war. Thousands of new jobs opened up in the sleepy town of Childersburg near Birmingham when Du-Pont built the $70 million Alabama Ordnance Works there. Tent camps housed some workers while others commuted from the Birmingham area. Also, the Magic City once again saw its steel mills working around the clock. Artillery shells, bomb casings, and steel for ships that were built in Mobile, Pascagoula, and Decatur rolled out of Birmingham's factories. Hundreds of B-29 bombers were modified at the Bechtel-McCone Plant at the city's municipal airport. TCI was one of the nation's largest defense contractors; its Fairfield steel plant alone produced more than five million artillery shells.

In the Muscle Shoals area the abundant TVA electrical power brought new defense-related industries such as Union Carbide and Reynolds Metals. Reynolds built a plant to produce aluminum for defense contractors, and it was in operation by July 1941. Alabama's congressmen and senators who had supported Roosevelt throughout the 1930s were instrumental in getting government installa-tions and defense contracts for their state. In addition to politics, though, transportation improvements including nearly 4,500 miles of recently paved roads, excellent shipping facilities on the Tennessee and Black Warrior rivers, and the well-equipped port of Mobile also made Alabama an attractive site for such installations. The state had abundant power from privately owned Alabama Power Company and TVA and an ample supply of labor. Paradoxically, the latter was partially a result of the lingering depression in rural Alabama and neighboring states that the New Deal had not managed to erase.

The growth of defense industries and military facilities that began in the late 1930s meant that job opportunities soon became available for women and eventually for blacks as well. This situation was especially true after 1941 when Congress enacted the nation's first peacetime military draft law. By 1945 250,000 Alabamians would have served in the armed forces. Filling their places on the "home front" required the training of women and, under pressure from the federal government, blacks. Black Alabamians were barred from most defense contracts except as unskilled laborers until 1943 when NAACP lobbying forced the Fair Employment Practices Commission to require nondiscriminatory hiring by defense contractors. Compliance with this requirement sparked a two-day riot in May 1943 at the Alabama Dry Dock and Shipbuilding Company in Mobile when the company promoted a dozen blacks to positions as welders in segregated units. But the FEPC ruling meant that black Alabamians had unprecedented employment opportunities during the remainder of the war. In addition to learning new skills, they worked for higher wages than ever before. To a lesser extent this development was true for all workers, especially women. Teachers, retail workers, and farmers flocked to the new defense jobs, which paid far more than they had ever earned before. Most defense contractors also had to train a large percentage of their new employees. Until wartime rationing limited the availability of many consumer goods, the defense payrolls resulted in booming retail sales. Even during the war there was a thriving black market in commodities such as gasoline. Alabamians employed as war workers found themselves in the unusual position of having money to spend but very little on which to spend it. One result was the phenomenal sale of war bonds. More than $1.25 billion in bonds were purchased in the state. Per capita sales were higher in Alabama than any other state of the Union. Remembering the hard times before the war, Alabamians were saving money when they had it. The average industrial wage doubled and the total industrial payroll tripled by the end of the war. In 1945, for the first time in the state's history, more Alabamians worked in industry than on farms. Those who remained on the land also prospered, although less dramatically than urban workers. Each year after 1941 the value of all agricultural products increased while the acreage devoted to farming declined. Fewer farmers made more money from less farmland. Cotton production remained high, but increasing emphasis was placed on livestock, corn, and truck farming. The percentage of tenants decreased steadily from its mid-1930s high of 64 percent of all farmers. Farmers also used greater quantities of fertilizer, much of it coming from the TVA-operated nitrate plants at Muscle Shoals.

Although World War II pumped billions of dollars into the state and changed the way all Alabamians lived, the conflict affected no city more than Mobile. Before the war Mobile's work force, excluding domestics, had numbered 17,000. By 1943 Brookley Field alone employed nearly that many civilians and the shipyards more than 40,000 other workers. Between 1940 and 1943, an estimated 89,000 people came to the Port City looking for work. The influx of newcomers overwhelmed every public service, including police and fire protection, medical services, education, housing, and even the municipal water and sewage systems. Schools went on double shifts, juvenile delinquency and truancy were rampant, and venereal disease rates rose alarmingly.

Despite the difficulties resulting from the sudden doubling of the area's population, Alabama Dry Dock and Shipbuilding Company (ADDSCO), Bender, and Gulf Shipyards built 192 ships during the war, or an average of one vessel a week. In addition ADDSCO alone repaired and refitted more than 2,800 other ships. The state docks handled vast quantities of war matériel throughout the conflict.

Although some Mobilians were critical of the manners and morals of the newly arrived workers, most of whom came from rural areas, few wanted to see the city return to its prewar torpor. Throughout Alabama the consensus was that the wartime prosperity must continue after the conflict's end. Too many Alabamians, male and female, black and white, had enjoyed prosperity beyond anything they might have imagined just a decade earlier; they would not give it up without a struggle. Black Alabamians especially were determined to hold on to the economic gains they had achieved and to press for political and social progress as well. After the war, returning black servicemen joined in the struggle against segregation, basing their demands for equality on the very democratic principles the United States had been fighting to protect.

When the Japanese surrendered in August 1945, Alabamians joined their fellow citizens in celebration. Although the end of the war meant the loss of many defense jobs, and indeed many already had ended, the state had received billions of dollars in capital investment, most of which would find peacetime use. Federal and state authorities also had undertaken measures to avoid the economic depression that had followed the end of World War I. Alabamians were optimistic that, having survived the virtual collapse of the old agricultural system, the Great Depression, and two wars, they could make the transition to a prosperous postwar economy. Indeed, they looked forward to the end of rationing and the resumption of peacetime production of cars, household appliances, and consumer goods in general. As they celebrated the end of the war, Alabamians anticipated a future in the mainstream of American life as full participants in the nation's prosperity and no longer as the poor country relations. Black Alabamians were as determined as their white compatriots to achieve their goal of full equality. In fact, their struggle already had begun, but few whites anticipated the importance of the issue of civil rights in Alabama's future or the role that the state would play in the ensuing national struggle. At the end of the summer of 1945, it was enough that the war and the depression were over. For most Alabamians, black or white, the future had never looked so good.

Photographs

For some time before the United States entered World War I on the Allied side in 1917, Alabamians had supported such a step. Once in the conflict, parades were held in cities and towns across the state to demonstrate home front support for the boys "over there." This Liberty Bond parade on Government Street in Mobile captures the patriotic spirit of the times. Erik Overbey photograph. (University of South Alabama Photographic Archives)

Alabamians flocked to the army, navy, and marine recruiters. Nearly 95,000 of the state's young men served during World War I. Their enthusiasm for military service probably reflected the state's economic woes in addition to its citizens' patriotic sentiments. These wartime marine recruiters were photographed in Birmingham by O. V. Hunt. (Birmingham Public Library)

Students at the state's colleges and universities also were affected by the war. Many joined officer training programs on their campuses. Here student soldiers at the University of Alabama do calisthenics in 1918 under the watchful eye of their officers. (The University of Alabama, Special Collections)

Although the United States entered the war with the aim of making the world safe for democracy, it continued to practice racial segregation at all levels in its domestic life. Despite this national pattern of discrimination, black students at Tuskegee Institute joined the army during the war and prepared to fight their country's battles in its segregated units. (Tuskegee Institute Archives)

928-A   N.A. TRAINING BRANCH - TUSKEGEE INST., ALA.

On their way to war, recruits were transported by trains they had decorated with appropriate graffiti. Alabama's soldiers participated in several major battles, but the ferocity and carnage of the trenches were apparently far from the minds of these young men. (Alabama Department of Archives and History)

Patriotic spirits were kept high on the home front with pageants extolling the lofty ideals of President Wilson's Fourteen Points. Here Miss Liberty brings hope to the oppressed Europeans in a patriotic tableau produced by the Noble Institute for Girls in Anniston, Alabama. (Anniston–Calhoun County Public Library)

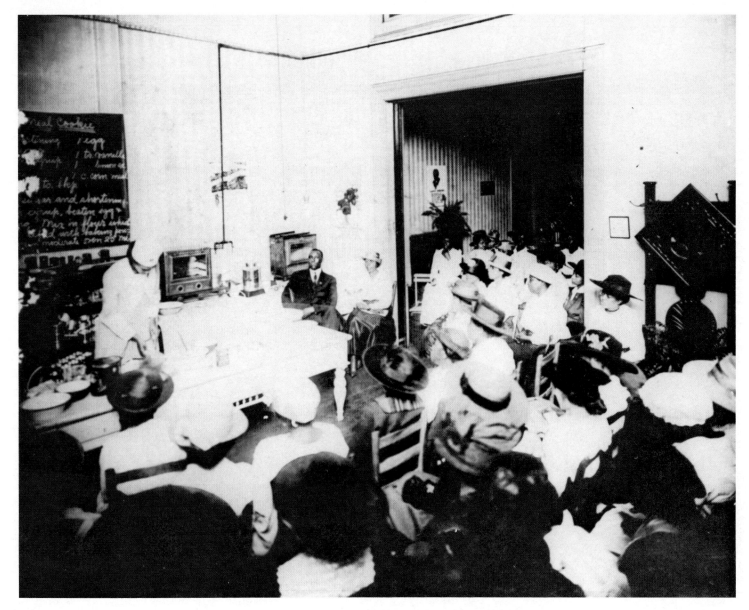

Black Alabamians also were involved in the war effort on the home front. In March 1918 a "War Kitchen" was opened for black women in Montgomery under the auspices of the Alabama Polytechnic Institute (later Auburn University and hereafter so cited) and the United States Department of Agriculture. Its purpose was to provide instruction in the preparation of nutritious and balanced meals, despite wartime shortages, to the women who traditionally did much of the cooking in southern homes and institutions. (Auburn University Archives)

The state's various ethnic groups also endeavored to associate themselves with the country's lofty war aims. The children of the Italian Society of Birmingham on this float represented boys and girls of many lands surrounding a young lady symbolizing the United States. Italy was on the Allied side, but Americans of German origin (and there were many in Alabama) could do little more than keep a low profile. O. V. Hunt photograph. (Birmingham Public Library, Archives and Manuscripts)

Alabama's women served the war effort in many ways—working in jobs previously held by men, serving in armed forces auxiliary units, and undertaking a variety of volunteer services. The American Red Cross maintained this canteen next to Montgomery's Union Station. As was true of similar establishments in other cities in the state, it was a haven for traveling servicemen. This picture was made at the canteen on July 31, 1919, when some American servicemen were just getting home from "over there." (Alabama Department of Archives and History)

Women serving in the Motor Corps Division, National League for Women's Service, worked with soldiers recovering from wounds received in battle. Twice each week they drove men from Montgomery's Camp Sheridan to this private residence for fresh air and refreshments. (Alabama Department of Archives and History)

Despite the overtime occasioned by dramatic increases in wartime orders for iron and steel, the people of Birmingham found time for recreation. Even in tree-shaded Eastlake Park, the war and the home front's desire to know more about it intruded in the form of a diorama of one of that conflict's major battles involving American forces—the Battle of the Argonne, which finally was ended by the armistice itself. O. V. Hunt photograph. (Birmingham Public Library, Archives and Manuscripts)

In Europe Alabamians contributed to the war effort in a variety of ways. General William Crawford Gorgas, a Mobile native, was the United States Surgeon General during the war. His medical work in France earned him recognition by the French government. In this photograph, made in 1919, General Gorgas was invested with his insignia as a commander in the Legion of Honor. (Alabama Department of Archives and History)

No city in Alabama felt the impact of the war more than Mobile, where orders for all types of ships suddenly increased when the United States entered the conflict. In 1916 the Alabama Dry Dock and Shipbuilding Company had been formed, and business boomed during the war. This photograph shows the launching of the SS *Houston,* a cargo vessel at ADDSCO, in 1918. Erik Overbey photograph. (University of South Alabama Photographic Archives)

ADDSCO was not Mobile's only shipyard. In 1914 Tennessee Coal and Iron Company, a subsidiary of U.S. Steel, had begun construction of a shipyard at Chickasaw, north of Mobile. The SS *Mobile City,* shown here just after its launching in 1920, was a World War I project, but the unexpected German surrender ended the war before the vessel was completed. Mobile's shipyards also built large wooden and even concrete hulled ships, but the abrupt end of the war halted these experiments. Erik Overbey photograph. (University of South Alabama Photographic Archives)

At Muscle Shoals in north Alabama the war brought the largest federal project ever undertaken in the state. As authorized by the National Defense Act of 1916, the government began the Wilson Dam on the Tennessee River and two associated plants that were designed to produce nitrate necessary for wartime gunpowder and fertilizer to increase domestic agricultural production. Black and white workers required for the construction of the nitrate plants and dam were housed in barracks, fed from mess halls, and provided with recreation facilities, all of which were segregated. The photograph on this page shows the pantry for Nitrate Plant #2, while that on the facing page shows the adjacent recreation hall provided for black workers. Despite segregation's Jim Crow laws, federal jobs paid blacks very well by local standards. (Tennessee Valley Authority, National Fertilizer Development Center)

A-132
COLORED RECREATION HALL
G-7
U.S.N.P. #2
MUSCLE SHOALS ALA.

33

The armistice ending the Great War was celebrated joyfully throughout Alabama. White workers at Nitrate Plant #2 celebrated victory with a minstrel show on November 12, 1918, the day after the armistice was signed. Although the plants at Muscle Shoals were finished before the end of World War I, they did not go into production and the area's hopes for economic development built around them and the Wilson Dam were dashed. (Tennessee Valley Authority, National Fertilizer Development Center)

In Mobile, where the armistice also would mean a sharp blow to the city's wartime economic prospects, news of the war's end was received just before dawn on November 11. The whole day was given over to celebration, parades, and impromptu floats, one of which proposed to hang the kaiser. However, the dominant emotion was not vengeance but relief that the killing had stopped. This photograph shows some of the 10,000 people who jammed the city's streets that day. Erik Overbey photograph. (University of South Alabama Photographic Archives)

In May 1919, more than six months after the armistice, Alabama's 167th Regiment finally returned home, marching through cheering crowds at every stop it made. This photo by O. V. Hunt was taken on 20th Street in Birmingham. (Birmingham Public Library, Archives and Manuscripts)

After their reception in the
Magic City, the 167th Regiment went to Montgomery
where on May 12 its men
were mustered out of service.
Their welcome in the capital
included a triumphal arch,
girls throwing flowers in their
path, and streets thronged
with well-wishers. (Alabama
Department of Archives and
History)

If some Alabamians nostalgically longed for a return to "normalcy" after the war, many of the state's women did not. They fought for women's suffrage, as indeed they had been doing for many years. In voting after the war, Alabama and the South (except Tennessee) declined to ratify the Nineteenth Amendment despite the efforts of suffragists such as these from the Birmingham state headquarters. Nevertheless, the constitutional amendment, which had widespread support outside the South, was adopted. (Alabama Department of Archives and History)

After the suffrage amendment became part of the Constitution in August 1920, women registered to vote across Alabama in scenes such as this one in Mobile. The franchise extension did not usher in a political revolution or lead to the destruction of family life, as some had feared. Unfortunately, it also did not noticeably raise the tone of Alabama's politics as some had hoped. Erik Overbey photograph. (University of South Alabama Photographic Archives)

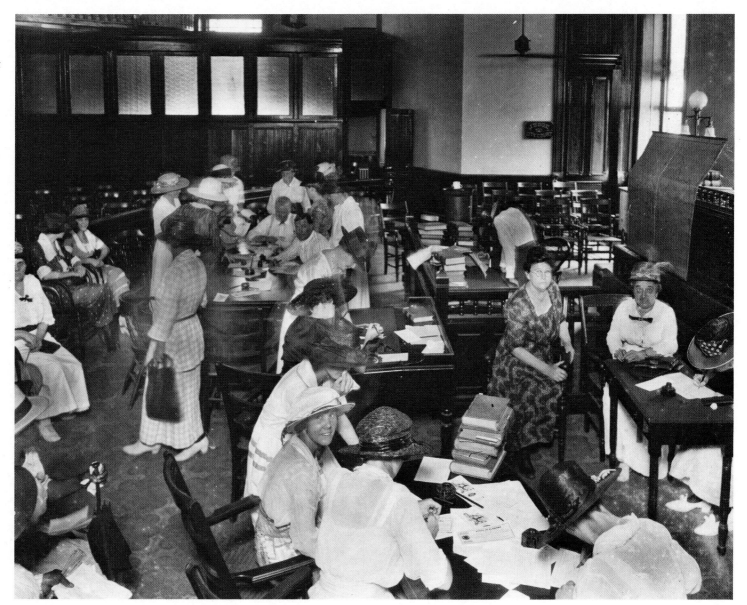

Postwar political issues were forgotten when the shrimp boats came in from Mobile Bay and the Gulf of Mexico with their loads; everyone pitched in to head the shrimp and ice them down. Seafood was one of coastal Alabama's biggest money earners, and shrimping was also a popular avocation of many residents of Mobile and Baldwin counties. These photos were made at Dauphin Island in the early 1920s. (Alabama Department of Archives and History)

In Alabama's smaller towns recreation took a variety of forms, most of which required little or no capital outlay. But small-town Alabama was not immune to national fads. For example, the craze for the pogo stick, which swept America in the Roaring Twenties, struck Gadsden. In this photograph by Albert Lebourg, a young man springs along the town's sidewalk in August 1922. (Frank Lebourg, Gadsden)

Another diversion was provided by the street vendors and musicians who were a common sight throughout Alabama. In this Erik Overbey photo, which was made in Mobile, a blind musician plays a sort of pipe organ/calliope. He was a fixture on downtown streets for many years. Most cities and towns had at least one "interesting" street person or local "character" to add spice to the everyday pattern of life. (University of South Alabama Photographic Archives)

Clubs went on excursions into the countryside during the early 1920s. Here, members of the Gadsden Motorcycle Club enjoy a beer on their outing to Glencoe. Prohibition seems to have had very limited impact upon their behavior. Albert Lebourg photograph. (Frank Lebourg, Gadsden)

Local daredevils also offered a break in the everyday routine. Albert Lebourg photographed this intrepid spirit at each of two separate jumps from the Gadsden post office building in the 1920s. Such demonstrations of bravado brought out the crowds in towns small and large. The same stuntman successfully crossed nearby Noccalula Falls on a high wire on another occasion. (Frank Lebourg, Gadsden)

In the countryside many Alabamians turned to hunting, especially in the fall and early winter. Some hunted for sport while others went out for "the pot." It was not at all uncommon for returning hunters such as these to be photographed with their trophies before the game was dressed. (The University of Alabama, Special Collections)

Picnics were also a popular form of recreation throughout the state. Because they were held outdoors, everyone could be accommodated with a minimum of fuss. Albert Lebourg made this photograph one Decoration Day in the early 1920s at the Macedonia Methodist Church in Dogwood, Alabama, near Alabaster. In the company of food, family, and friends, the time was passed with all-day singing and other activities. (Frank Lebourg, Gadsden)

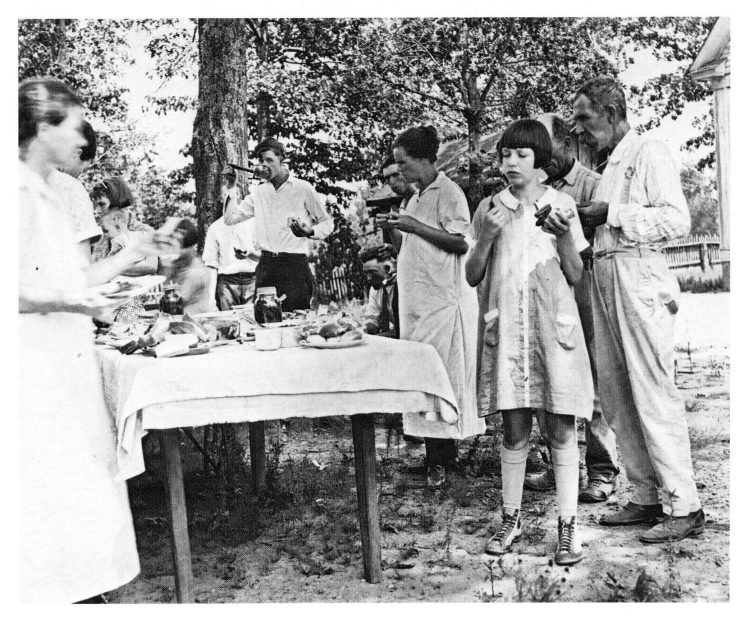

Some large textile mills arranged to take all their employees on an annual picnic in the country. The Merrimack Manufacturing Company in Huntsville chartered railway cars to transport its employees to the company picnic. In the Huntsville area two of the favorite destinations were the site of the old Bell Factory or the Three Forks of the Flint River. The children waded in the creeks until dinner was spread out on cloths under the trees. A company's altruism in making such a holiday possible was reinforced by its desire to avoid the unionization of its workers. (Huntsville–Madison County Public Library)

In the 1920s Alabama's smaller towns were filled with people from the surrounding countryside, especially on Saturdays, despite the state's indifferent road system. Although the streetcar is prominent in this picture of Florence in 1920, the number of cars indicates that the automobile rapidly was becoming the preferred means of travel for those who could afford it. G. W. Landrum photograph. (Jerry Landrum, Florence)

One of the attractions of the town was the curb markets where farmers sold fresh produce off the backs of their trucks and wagons. This curb market was in Tuscaloosa, but similar scenes were to be found throughout the state. (Auburn University Archives)

The Catanzano Brothers in Birmingham ran a typical grocery store before the age of the supermarket. Groceries like the Catanzanos' existed throughout the state, but national and regional retail chains began to challenge such establishments during the interwar years. O. V. Hunt photograph. (Birmingham Public Library, Archives and Manuscripts)

As traditional in its way as the Catanzano Brothers' Grocery, Rosen's store on Second Avenue, Bessemer, pictured here, sold men's clothing in surroundings that looked as if they were lifted straight out of the 1890s. Blacks and whites often shopped at the same stores, although with their lower pay scales black workers and their families could afford to buy much less. The pace of life was reflected in Mr. Rosen's sign, "If you don't decide today, we will be here tomorrow." (Bessemer Hall of History Museum)

For blacks in Alabama economic opportunities were severely limited, even in the cities. Women could work as domestics, men as laborers. Skilled positions such as barbers, teamsters, and masons, once filled by blacks, were being taken over by whites after the war. Shining shoes remained one of the services blacks traditionally provided whites, whether it was boys on the street or men in a shoe-shine parlor. O. V. Hunt photographs. (Birmingham Public Library, Archives and Manuscripts)

Alabama's black population survived the strictures of segregation by working for improved educational opportunities to shield their children from the double blows of racism and ignorance. The photo here, made in 1922, shows the unveiling of the statue of Booker T. Washington at Tuskegee Institute. The monument commemorated the leadership that the man and the institute had provided black Alabama. (Tuskegee Institute Archives)

In 1919 the farmers of Coffee County, led by Enterprise city councilman R. O. Fleming, erected a monument of a different sort, honoring the boll weevil. The agricultural diversification that resulted from the insect's destruction of cotton crops was the reason for such an unusual tribute. (Auburn University Archives)

The early 1920s was not a time of great innovation in the cities, towns, and countryside of Alabama. Conservative business interests in the larger cities were disinclined to change the status quo. They were concerned about the transition to "normalcy," and they were comfortable in a lifestyle that included business dinners such as this one, enjoyed by executives of the Birmingham Paper Company, at the elegant Tutwiler Hotel in 1924. (Birmingham Public Library, Archives and Manuscripts)

Conservatives also demanded frugality in state government. Dr. Thomas M. Owen, shown here at his desk in the Alabama Department of Archives and History in the fall of 1918, had led the successful fight to establish the department in 1901. This precedent-setting step was not followed by adequate funding. Dr. Owen continued to labor in crowded conditions in the old state capitol for the rest of his life. After his death on March 25, 1920, his wife succeeded him as director of the department and held the post for the next thirty-five years. (Alabama Department of Archives and History)

Despite the conservative spirit of the times, changes were coming. Radio made its first, albeit tentative, invasion of Alabama's homes and businesses in the 1920s. This photo shows W. A. Young broadcasting a baseball game on WAPI, Auburn, in April 1928. The station later moved to Birmingham. Radios were expensive and cantankerous and there were few stations until the 1930s. Only fifteen stations operated in the state in 1940. If Alabamians really wanted to follow baseball, they went to the ball park in person. (Auburn University Archives)

The state's major cities had minor league ball clubs. In the spring major league teams visited to play exhibition games. Babe Ruth and the Yankees came to Mobile on several occasions, playing at Monroe Park and Hartwell Field to the delight of young and old alike. Here the "Sultan of Swat" meets some of his younger fans. Erik Overbey photograph. (University of South Alabama Photographic Archives)

In addition to exhibition baseball games, springtime also meant pageants, which were put on by schools, churches, and the larger mines and mills throughout the state. The Spring Festival of 1928 portraying Old King Cole and his retinue featured white children of employees of the Tennessee Coal and Iron Company. (Birmingham Public Library, Archives and Manuscripts) In the Woodward Iron Company festival of the same year, three women are clouds. (The University of Alabama, Special Collections)

1149

The paternalism of large corporations such as the Tennessee Coal and Iron Company, spurred on by fears of labor unrest, sometimes included caring for employees' children while parents worked. All aspects of life in the TCI village, adjacent to the Muscoda ore mines, were segregated and under company control. However, white children did get a hot meal in decent surroundings, and more remarkable yet was the well-equipped kindergarten for black children. Both of these photographs were made for TCI in 1917. (The University of Alabama, Special Collections)

5-LD.

10-3.

65

Even the garden plots worked by schoolchildren were racially segrated. The white school at TCI's Blocton coal mine had its own garden, which was carefully tended by the children. The produce helped improve the poor diet that generally prevailed among miners and their families. (Birmingham Public Library, Archives and Manuscripts)

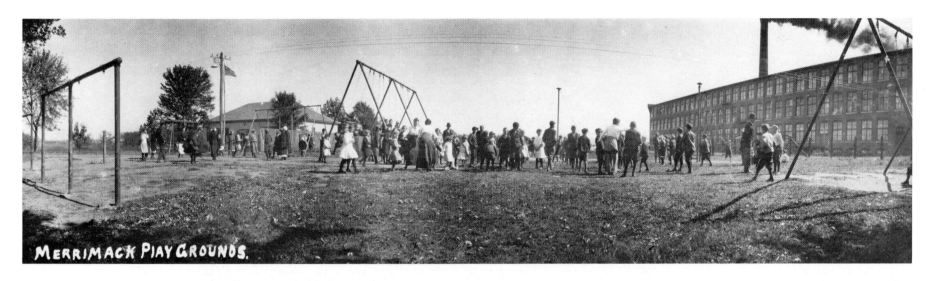

MERRIMACK PLAY GROUNDS.

Children throughout Alabama were handicapped by poor recreational and educational facilities. Often only the mines and mills provided such facilities and their use was limited to children of employees. The Merrimack playground in Huntsville was immediately adjacent to the mill where the children's parents worked. Some children worked in the state's textile mills before child labor came to an end in the late 1920s. (H. E. Monroe, Huntsville)

Provision for intellectual development also lagged in the state. For example, few Alabamians had access to a decent library. The gap was partially filled in Jefferson County by a bookmobile. In this photo it had stopped at the Sayre commissary station in the western part of the county in the late 1920s. (Birmingham Public Library, Archives and Manuscripts)

A much larger crowd welcomed the arrival of the same vehicle when it stopped at the Mount Olive Consolidated School, also in the late 1920s. A concerted effort was made during Bibb Graves's administration to replace one-room schools with modern consolidated facilities. (Alabama Department of Archives and History)

Although financial support for public education at all levels had been historically inadequate, Alabama had a system of higher education that could be traced back to the state's founding in 1819. The capstone of the system was the University of Alabama, located in Tuscaloosa, where students lived in rooms any undergraduate would recognize. This picture was taken in 1917 in Garland Hall. (The University of Alabama, Special Collections)

In an effort to attract returning veterans after the war,
the University of Alabama offered special programs under
the auspices of the Federal
Bureau of Vocational Education. In this 1921 photo students at the university were
learning the repair and main-
tenance of steam locomotives
by using a working model.
(The University of Alabama,
Special Collections)

Class In Machine Shop Practice—
Locomotives.
Students. F. B. V. E.
U. of A. Tuscaloosa. Ala. 6-30-21.

The University of Alabama's cross-state rival, Alabama Polytechnic Institute (Auburn), continued its emphasis on the sciences, particularly those relating to agriculture. These students are in the entomology class in Comer Hall in the early 1920s. Although overwhelmingly a male institution, Auburn was a coed school and there is a female in this picture. However, few of Alabama's young women received a higher education and most of those who did went to Normal or teacher-training institutions. (Auburn University Archives)

In addition to the opportunity for a formal education, college gave students the chance to meet nationally known personalities. In March 1928 Will Rogers visited Auburn and was escorted on the campus by a good-humored collection of students and townspeople. His speech that evening filled Smith Hall with an audience that included Governor Bibb Graves. Many students, unable to find seats inside, stood listening through the windows. In this photo the humorist is pictured with Colonel B. Anderson and an assortment of fans on the day of Rogers's arrival. (Auburn University Archives)

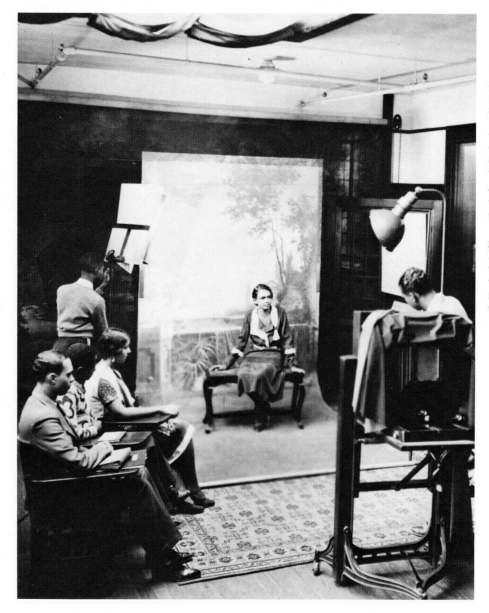

One of Alabama's most famous schools was Tuskegee Institute. Chartered by the state but supported primarily by the gifts of white philanthropists throughout the nation who were attracted by the philosophy of Booker T. Washington, it was a black coeducational college devoted to "practical" training. In this picture, made in the 1920s, students learn photographic technique from P. H. Polk, the now-legendary photographer of black Alabama who worked at Tuskegee for many years. (Tuskegee Institute Archives)

Tuskegee also offered a wide range of academic courses, including the chemistry class shown in this picture. However, it was the emphasis on employment-oriented education that distinguished Booker T. Washington and Tuskegee's approach to the problems facing blacks in a segregated society. (Tuskegee Institute Archives)

In the 1920s a barrier to Alabama's economic progress was its transportation system, particularly its road network. The prewar Good Roads Movement had effected some improvement in the state's highways, as indicated by this picture made near Florence. However, far more remained to be done, especially in the expensive job of building bridges across the state's many rivers. G. W. Landrum photograph. (Jerry Landrum, Florence)

Scenes such as this one were all too common, as a group of cars cross a river on a hand-operated ferry. The condition of the spare tire at the extreme right of the picture suggests the quality of Alabama's rural roads after World War I. (Alabama Department of Archives and History)

Road and bridge building were popular policies of Progressives, including Governor Bibb Graves, who became one of the state's leading road builders. He is shown here in 1927 dedicating the Broad Street bridge in Gadsden. Graves's administration saw a $25 million bond issue enacted with a state gasoline tax of two cents per gallon to pay for new roads and bridges. Albert Lebourg photograph. (Frank Lebourg, Gadsden)

The John T. Milner Bridge across the Tombigbee River in Pickens County, shown at its dedication in the late 1920s, was an example of the success achieved during the decade in road and bridge building. (Alabama Department of Archives and History)

The most ambitious highway project in Alabama in the decade was the Cochrane Bridge across Mobile Bay. Built with money raised by the sale of bonds in a plan developed by John T. Cochrane, the causeway and bridge system linking Mobile and Baldwin counties was completed in June 1927. In this picture Governor Graves and other notables pose for the photographers at the dedication ceremonies. Erik Overbey photograph. (University of South Alabama Photographic Archives)

A long line of cars waited to cross the new causeway on its opening day. The $10 million Cochrane Bridge, as the whole project was then known, was a great economic boost for Mobile and south Alabama, but it doomed the romantic old bayboats to extinction. Erik Overbey photograph. (University of South Alabama Photographic Archives)

In addition to road-building projects, the coming of the automobile required the development of an adequate network of service and repair facilities. The first garages were primitive affairs, often run by former blacksmiths. This one was the Dennis Tire Company in Bessemer, photographed on New Year's Eve 1919. (Bessemer Hall of History Museum)

A variety of auto-related jobs were available in new-car dealerships. A far cry from the old blacksmith shop, the modern dealer had tempting displays of new cars in a clean and well-organized environment. Pictured here is the parts department of Long-Lewis Ford in Bessemer, where the dealership's last Model A was on display in 1931. (Bessemer Hall of History Museum)

A demand for properly trained mechanics grew as automobiles became more numerous during the 1920s. To meet this demand the public schools in Birmingham offered auto-shop instruction at several locations by 1931, including the Paul Hayne School shown here. (Birmingham Public Library, Archives and Manuscripts)

Students at Tuskegee Institute also studied auto mechanics. Although black Alabamians historically had supplied many of the state's skilled artisans, these students would have a harder time finding good jobs than their white counterparts because of their race. (Tuskegee Institute Archives)

As the number of cars increased so did the frequency of wrecks. Some were more spectacular than others, but few were as dramatic as this single-car accident in Mobile. Erik Overbey photograph. (University of South Alabama Photographic Archives)

In the cities the cars contended with draft animals, narrow streets, and streetcars. This photograph, made in Mobile in 1925 by Erik Overbey, graphically illustrates the problems early motorists faced in dealing with the railed vehicles. (University of South Alabama Photographic Archives)

Whatever the urban hazards, those Alabamians who could afford a car regularly enjoyed jaunts through the countryside or quiet picnics away from it all. These pictures, made by Albert Lebourg near Gadsden in the early 1920s, illustrate the power and impact of technological change and how it had begun to affect the everyday lives of the people of Alabama. (Frank Lebourg, Gadsden)

Most Alabamians did not own cars during the interwar years. However, there was widespread fascination with the new technology and its various applications. In the mid-1920s, this "driverless" car passed through Birmingham on a cross-country promotion, and large crowds gathered to see the curiosity. (Birmingham Public Library, Archives and Manuscripts)

This photo was taken on October 5, 1927, as Charles Lindbergh, riding in the automobile at the left of the picture, entered Birmingham. His motorcade was cheered by crowds gathered to celebrate his historic trans-Atlantic flight. After his return to the United States, "Lucky Lindy" flew the "Spirit of St. Louis" around the country to publicize civil aviation and its potential benefits. He was welcomed as an authentic hero whose exploits modern technology had helped make possible. (Birmingham Public Library, Archives and Manuscripts)

Charles Lindbergh's visit to Birmingham was not the first occasion the Magic City had to show its interest in aviation. Earlier in the decade cross-country balloon races passed over the city. These photos show balloons in a 1920 race and the crew of a navy dirigible that had come up from the Pensacola Naval Air Station in 1923 to publicize another race. (Birmingham Public Library, Archives and Manuscripts)

Technology in the form of motion pictures molded patterns of behavior and reflected the tastes of the era with uncanny accuracy. *The Iron Horse*, shown in Birmingham within three months of its Hollywood opening in 1924, was a popular adventure tale. If the local girls did not make very convincing Indians, they did add the required promotional hoopla. O. V. Hunt photograph. (Birmingham Public Library, Archives and Manuscripts)

The modernism of the Roaring Twenties, with flappers, Prohibition, and speakeasies, was another expression of that era's fascination with technology and "progress." This photo by Erik Overbey of the mysterious Mardi Gras revelers in Mobile suggests that "anything goes" was more than a phrase in a popular song. (University of South Alabama Photographic Archives)

If the sinful diversions of the flapper era were to be found mainly in Alabama's cities, the power of the religious establishments there should not be underestimated. The Catholic church in Alabama was often a target for the Ku Klux Klan and some Prohibitionist and Protestant groups, but it remained a powerful force especially in Mobile and Birmingham. This photo by Erik Overbey shows the altar of the Cathedral of the Immaculate Conception in Mobile. The dignitaries in the procession include the longtime bishop of Mobile, the Most Reverend Thomas J. Toolen. (University of South Alabama Photographic Archives)

Most Alabamians did not share the cultural values and lifestyle symbolized by the term "Roaring Twenties." Along with the majority of Protestants, the state's Baptists (Alabama's largest denomination) were wary of temptation, favored Prohibition, and stressed the need for regular church attendance. The First Baptist Church in Birmingham broadcast its services on the radio while continuing to fill its Sunday school with youngsters such as these photographed in 1926. (Birmingham Public Library, Archives and Manuscripts)

In rural Alabama religious activity often spilled out of the small country church, sometimes leading to a baptism in a nearby river. This congregation in Lowndes County was black, but belief in baptism by immersion knew no racial barriers. Most black Alabamians were fundamentalists and Protestants, as were most whites, and religion was an important source of comfort in hard times to members of both races. (Alabama Department of Archives and History)

Motivated by the precepts of the social gospel, many Christian denominations undertook various domestic charities and preaching missions. In Birmingham one of the best known clerics was Brother Bryan of the Second Presbyterian Church. He regularly preached to people where they worked, such as police officers, firemen, and mill workers. In a textile mill, probably Avondale, Bryan is standing at the upper left, surrounded by women whose toil his sermon has interrupted. (Birmingham Public Library, Archives and Manuscripts)

Iron and steel were the mainstays of Birmingham's economy in the 1920s. Although handicapped by railroad freight charges and U.S. Steel's policies favoring its Pittsburgh mills, the Magic City was busy throughout most of the Roaring Twenties. This night shot of the Sloss Furnace at work symbolized the optimism that many felt during the "Prosperity Decade." O. V. Hunt photograph. (Birmingham Public Library, Archives and Manuscripts)

The work in the coal mines
that supplied fuel for Birmingham's mills was dangerous and dirty. After the
power of the United Mine
Workers was broken in the
1919–20 strike, lives of the
mine workers, their homes,
schools, and the stores in
which they shopped remained
largely under the control of
the companies. Employers invested their money in im-
proving production with
devices such as a mechanical
loader to fill coal cars, shown
in this 1927 TCI photo. (Alabama Department of Archives
and History)

In the Tennessee Valley, the partially finished Wilson Dam and the nitrate plants near Muscle Shoals stood idle. Because World War I ended abruptly, the plants never went into production, and work on the dam was suspended in 1921, shortly after this picture of the construction of the powerhouse was made. (Tennessee Valley Authority, National Fertilizer Development Center)

In an effort to complete Wilson Dam and use its power to spark economic development in the Muscle Shoals area, Henry Ford was invited to visit. He did so in June and again in December 1921. In this photo, taken by G. W. Landrum on the later visit, Ford and Thomas A. Edison surveyed the prospects the Wilson Dam offered. Ford's proposal to buy the dam for virtually nothing was not accepted by the federal government and he withdrew his offer. His "Seventy-Five Mile City" never materialized. The industrial development of the Tennessee Valley lagged for another decade until rescued by FDR's New Deal. (Jerry Landrum, Florence)

Throughout the 1920s in south Alabama, the old riverboats continued to take cargo down to Mobile much as they had done since antebellum days. But cotton prices were generally depressed and the land was wearing out. Scenes such as this one at Selma, photographed in 1931, were much more the echo of the past than the wave of the future. (Birmingham Public Library, Archives and Manuscripts)

Along the state's Gulf coast, Mobile's fishing industry continued to thrive in the 1920s as improved transportation facilities by road and rail enlarged the market that the city served. But the seafood industry was only a small part, albeit a colorful one, of the Port City's economy. Erik Overbey made this photograph at the Star Fish and Oyster Company docks at the foot of Canal Street in Mobile as workers unloaded the day's catch of snapper. (University of South Alabama Photographic Archives)

Throughout the 1920s Mobile's economic leaders agressively sought industrial development for the city. Older firms such as the Kahn Overall Factory employed a large number of seamstresses who worked in conditions that were above average for the period. However, Mobile's economy was little more diversified than it had been in the late nineteenth century. Erik Overbey photograph. (University of South Alabama Photographic Archives)

A real change in Mobile's economic life came at the end of the decade with the opening of the International Paper Mill in 1928. The company had been courted artfully by the city's business leaders, and the new plant created hundreds of jobs in both the construction and the industrial fields. Erik Overbey photograph. (University of South Alabama Photographic Archives)

Although the coming of International Paper was an important step for Mobile, the city's growth was severely retarded by its antiquated port facilities. After years of intense lobbying by Mobilians, the Alabama State Docks was constructed on swampland north of the city at a cost to the state of $10 million. This photo by Erik Overbey shows the official dedication of the new facility on June 25, 1928. (University of South Alabama Photographic Archives)

In May 1927 the warehouses at the docks had not been finished when the first ships were unloaded. When completed, the Alabama State Docks was the most modern facility of its kind in the nation. Although serving agricultural and industrial interests throughout the state, no area benefited more from this investment of state capital than Mobile. Erik Overbey photograph. (University of South Alabama Photographic Archives)

Life in Mobile and other cities in Alabama offered a measure of sophistication and diversity that contrasted sharply with the state's rural areas. A wide assortment of goods and services was available along busy Dauphin Street, the center of retail trade in Mobile. Erik Overbey photograph. (University of South Alabama Photographic Archives)

Magazines and newspapers from all over the state and nation were available at Ben Fell's in Birmingham. City newsstands offered a variety of sources of information and points of view, but urban Alabama retained many of the values of the state's rural areas. O. V. Hunt photograph. (Birmingham Public Library, Archives and Manuscripts)

On the eve of World War I the Ku Klux Klan was revived in Georgia. By the mid-1920s the Klan had virtually taken over political life in the Birmingham area. Mass rallies and initiations, like these at Bessemer in 1925 (top) and Birmingham in 1924 (bottom), were regular events. Catholics, Jews, and blacks were harassed, intimidated, and killed by the hooded brotherhood. (Top photograph, Bessemer Hall of History Museum; bottom photograph, Birmingham Public Library, Archives and Manuscripts)

The Klan met and paraded
openly in towns and cities
throughout the state, including Montgomery, as shown
in this 1921 Confederate Veterans' parade. Fearful of its
power, most national, state,
and local officeholders in
Alabama knuckled under to
the Klan or openly courted
its support throughout most
of the 1920s. (Alabama Department of Archives and
History)

Aspiring politicians such as Hugo Black joined the Klan. Not to have done so would have meant the end of his promising political career. Black eventually publicly renounced the Klan in the 1930s after President Roosevelt had appointed him to the United States Supreme Court. This photograph of the Robert E. Lee Klavern to which Black belonged was made in the 1920s. (*Birmingham News*)

When Klan power and influence were at their height in Birmingham, its hooded members openly distributed information on the streets. Editorials by Grover Hall of the *Montgomery Advertiser* and a series of scandals brought an end to Klan power. However, much of the damage to lives and property caused by the organization could never be undone. (*Birmingham News*)

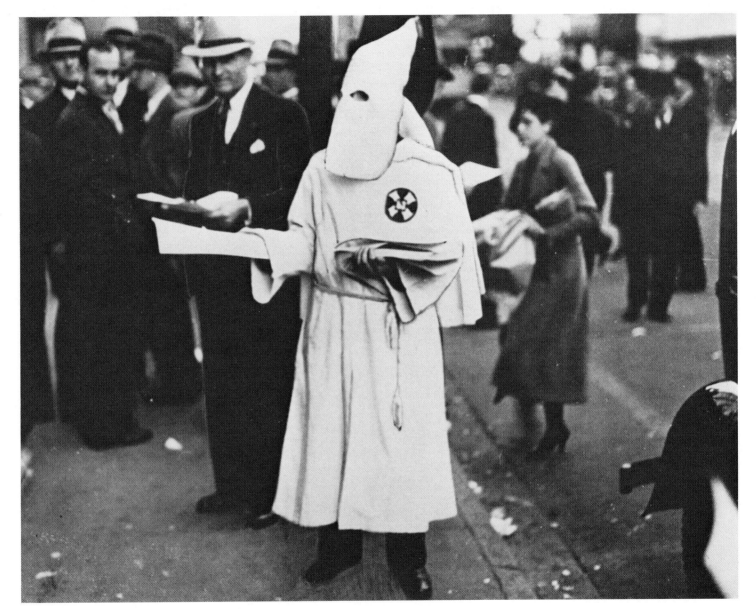

The Roaring Twenties or the "Prosperity Decade" failed to live up to its billing in rural Alabama. Still largely operating in an economy based on a single crop, cotton, conditions in the state's rural areas went from bad to worse. Landowners, such as those pictured on this page, made their profits from sharecropping or farm tenancy. (Auburn University Archives) The landowners's reluctance to see crop diversification meant that farmers, such as the couple in the P. H. Polk photograph on the facing page, would work longer and longer hours for less and less reward as their cotton planting wore out the land. (Tuskegee Institute Archives)

In an effort to improve productivity some farmers tried diversification and mechanization. The photo on this page shows an early tractor pulling a primitive combine through a hayfield in the Tennessee Valley. (H. E. Monroe, Huntsville) In the picture on the facing page, made in 1926, farmers in Baldwin County use a tractor to harvest Irish potatoes. (Auburn University Archives) While such experiments met with some success, the poverty of most farmers and the tenant farming/crop lien system militated against innovation.

The movable school, or Farmer's College, of Tuskegee Institute was an effort to bring practical education to the poorer farmers of Alabama. Its "Knapp Truck," shown here, traveled all over Macon County and beyond, bringing lessons on nutrition and hygiene to "the man furtherest down," in Booker T. Washington's words. The program, which received some state support, was begun in the 1890s in an effort to improve the quality of life among black farmers. (Tuskegee Institute Archives)

The Alabama Cooperative Extension Service was a larger effort with goals similar to those of the Farmer's College. In this photo a black extension agent demonstrates canning methods in Montgomery County. Given inadequate funding and the requirement that it maintain a segregated force, the extension service was hard pressed to meet the educational needs of the state's farmers, black and white. The poor quality of the state's rural roads made it difficult to reach some communities or to meet with more than a few farm families at a time. (Auburn University Archives)

Efforts to diversify the state's agricultural system included programs to upgrade poultry production. In this photograph, an Alabama Cooperative Extension Service agent inspects turkeys on the De-Sherbinin farm in Dallas County in 1927. This farm was one of the first to raise turkeys in Alabama. (Auburn University Archives)

In a far more typical rural scene, this elderly black man made baskets on the front porch of his cabin while a young child watched. No state agency taught him this skill, nor was there much economic reward for having it. Scenes such as this one, photographed by P. H. Polk in Macon County, were to be found throughout the state. (Tuskegee Institute Archives)

123

In her neat if spartan kitchen, a Franklin County woman uses a new faucet and sink made possible by a water system installed by the Cooperative Extension Service. The progress such programs achieved was insufficient to offset the fundamental problems faced by the state's agricultural system. (Auburn University Archives)

Not all of Alabama's smaller farmers gave up hope of making their farms work. The farmer keeping up his ledger in this Cooperative Extension Service photograph was putting into practice procedures taught to him by the service. (Auburn University Archives)

Even the elements seemed to conspire against Alabama as the 1920s ended. In March 1929 floods did widespread damage in southern Alabama. This aerial view of the city of Brewton shows the city center entirely underwater. Similar scenes were to be found elsewhere in the southern parts of the state. (Alabama Department of Archives and History)

The U.S. Army Air Corps
flew flood relief missions
from Maxwell Field to drop
supplies to areas isolated by
the rising waters. In this photograph soldiers loaded a
plane for a flight to the
flood-ravaged southern counties. (Maxwell Air Force
Base, Air University Office of
History)

At the end of the 1920s cotton prices fell dramatically. The more cotton Alabamians planted in an effort to pay their bills, the less each bale brought and the more devastated the land became. Publicity efforts designed to boost cotton prices or to draw attention to the farmer's plight had achieved nothing of consequence. This photograph was made in Birmingham by O. V. Hunt in the late teens or early twenties. (Birmingham Public Library, Archives and Manuscripts)

A modern bridge near Guntersville was one of the achievements of the Good Roads Movement. But the collapse of the Alabama farm economy, coupled with the Great Depression, gave the bridge a new role to play. It transported farmers fleeing the land with whatever possessions they could pile on their old cars. Such people had nowhere to go and no way to earn a living. As the unfulfilled promise of the "Prosperity Decade" evaporated, rural Alabamians would be hit harder by the depression than the average American. Albert Lebourg photograph. (Frank Lebourg, Gadsden)

For many who were homeless and jobless in the depression, the road and the roadside camp were home. In this 1937 photograph by Arthur Rothstein, the man is building a chair to sell to tourists or other passersby on the outskirts of Birmingham while living with his family in a roadside tent. (Library of Congress)

Many men and their families passed through Mobile searching for work. The Port City had no jobs for such transients or for the hoboes who lived in villages near the city's railroad yards and waterfront. Erik Overbey photograph. (University of South Alabama Photographic Archives)

Private religious and charitable organizations, notably the Salvation Army, did what they could to meet the human needs of Alabama's unemployed. In Mobile the Salvation Army ran a soup kitchen for transients and unemployed people. In Birmingham the city's colorful mayor, Jimmy Jones, contributed to the Salvation Army's Christmas kettles. But the need was far beyond the capacity of private charities to meet no matter how dedicated they were. Kitchen photograph by S. Blake McNeely. (University of South Alabama Photographic Archives) Jones photograph by O. V. Hunt. (Birmingham Public Library, Archives and Manuscripts)

In the 1930s, unemployed
men with nothing but time
on their hands were common
features throughout Alabama.
In Birmingham, the state's
(and the nation's) hardest-hit
city with over 25 percent unemployment, the mills were
shut down and workers
whiled away the hours on the
porches of run-down rooming
houses or in idle groups gathered on street corners. Both
photographs were made by
Walker Evans in 1936. (Library of Congress)

134

During the depression many older and poorer blue-collar neighborhoods deteriorated into slums similar to this block on Birmingham's south side. (Birmingham Public Library, Archives and Manuscripts)

In Mobile and other munici-
palities, destitute people also
lived in shantytowns they had
built in or near the local
dump where they foraged
food. Social problems such as
these, spawned by the na-
tion's economic collapse,
were beyond the ability of
Alabama's cities and towns
to handle. Even the state government lacked the necessary
resources to meet the challenge. Erik Overbey photograph. (University of South
Alabama Photographic Ar-
chives)

Those lucky enough to have jobs in a mine or mill lived in company houses located in company towns. The housing was often in poor repair, but the alternative was worse, inasmuch as losing the job meant losing the house. The dwellings in Walker Evans's 1936 photograph made in Birmingham were owned by Republic Steel. (Library of Congress)

The armed guard at a TCI village near Birmingham was on the lookout for labor violence, which hard times, company policies, and efforts to organize unions combined to create. Arthur Rothstein photographed this scene in 1936. (Library of Congress)

Demand for coal and iron collapsed during the depression. Thus, jobs in the mines were few and far between when this photo was made in 1931 by Fred A. Powell for the Sullivan Mine Machinery Company. (Jackie Dobbs, Old Birmingham Photographs)

Those who were employed were paid in either scrip or "clacker," redeemable only at the company store and usually at rates that favored the company. TCI's Ensley Store was typical of such establishments. (Library of Congress)

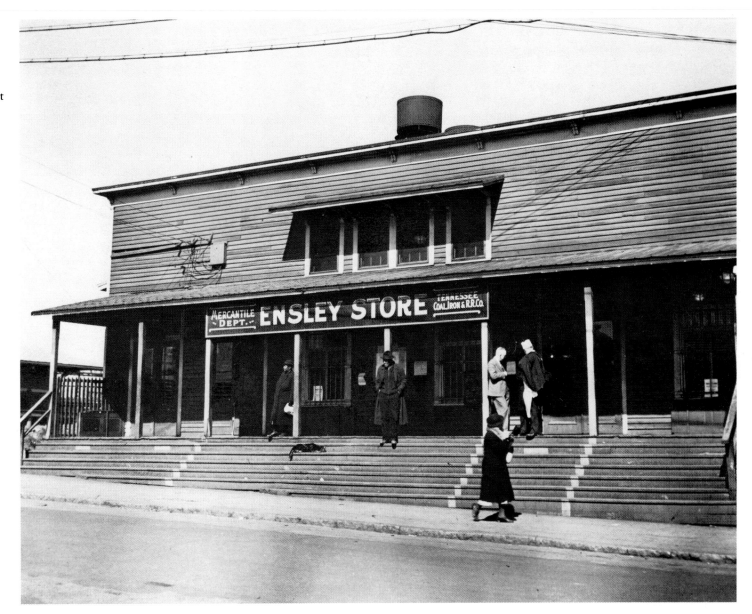

ELECTRIC FURNACE
KILBY CAR & FOUNDRY CO.
ANNISTON ALA MAY 19-1936

Men with industrial jobs often had to accept short time or substantial pay cuts to keep working during the depression. Even so, most people with steady employment counted themselves lucky. The group of men on this page was photographed in May 1936 at the Kilby Car and Foundry Company in Anniston. (Anniston–Calhoun County Public Library) The railway worker on the facing page, photographed by Arthur Rothstein, emerges from a cloud of steam escaping from a locomotive in Birmingham. (Library of Congress)

During the depression, free workers did not have to compete with state prisoners for jobs in the private sector because convict leasing by the state had been ended officially in 1927. However, convict labor on public projects continued to be used, and a disproportionate percentage of convicts were black. This road gang was photographed by Arthur Rothstein in Jefferson County in February 1935. (Library of Congress)

The bankruptcy of race relations in Alabama was evident in the story of the "Scottsboro Boys." Nine young black men hoboing on the L & N railroad in 1931 were arrested and charged with raping two white girls. Convicted repeatedly despite the evidence, and spared execution only by appeals to the United States Supreme Court, the "boys" made legal history but at the cost of years out of their lives. Here the defendants are being led out of the Decatur Courthouse during their second trial in 1933. Their treatment long served as a reminder to the rest of the nation of the racism of southern justice. (*Birmingham News*)

The people of rural Alabama were accustomed to lives filled with hard physical labor, but the collapse of cotton prices, which plummeted to five cents a pound in 1931, added despair to their burden. The black operator of the ferry at Gee's Bend on the Alabama River had little reason to hope for better times. Marion Post Wolcott photograph. (Library of Congress)

After years of overcropping, much of Alabama looked like this farm, which Arthur Rothstein photographed in 1937 near Birmingham. As a result of erosion such as that pictured here, significantly less arable land remained in the state in 1930 than had existed in 1920. (Library of Congress)

For generations Alabama's farmers had depended upon the light mule-drawn plow to prepare the soil for planting. Few knew anything of terracing, contour plowing, or fertilizing. Tenancy and the sharecropping system tied most of them to growing cotton, even as the price plummeted and the land was destroyed. This photo was taken in June 1936 by Dorothea Lange. The plowman earned seventy-five cents a day. (Library of Congress)

Although most sharecroppers were white, more than 80 percent of black farmers in Alabama were tenants with few resources beyond their own muscle power. In July 1936 Dorothea Lange photographed this family working in the fields near Eutaw. She entitled the picture "Hoe Culture in the South" in the report to the Farm Security Administration that accompanied her exposed film. (Library of Congress)

Many of the photographs made in Alabama in the 1930s have gone on to become famous as artistic documents that have made the period come alive for later generations. This photo taken by Arthur Rothstein of a young girl in Gee's Bend is an example of the phenomenon. (Library of Congress)

For every photograph that has become famous, there are a dozen that are less well known but still convey the hardships Alabamians endured. These children of a turpentine worker living near Cordele in 1936 were photographed by Dorothea Lange. She recorded that their father earned one dollar a day when he could find work. (Library of Congress)

The interior of the cabins of rural Alabama farmers varied in appearance, but at their best they reflected lives lived at a pitifully low level of material existence. The photo on this page was made in Greensboro in 1941 by Jack Delano. The people were tenant farmers. On the facing page is a photo made in 1939 by Marion Post Wolcott showing a more desperate family. The children had hookworm, the mother pellagra. Neither affliction was uncommon. (Library of Congress)

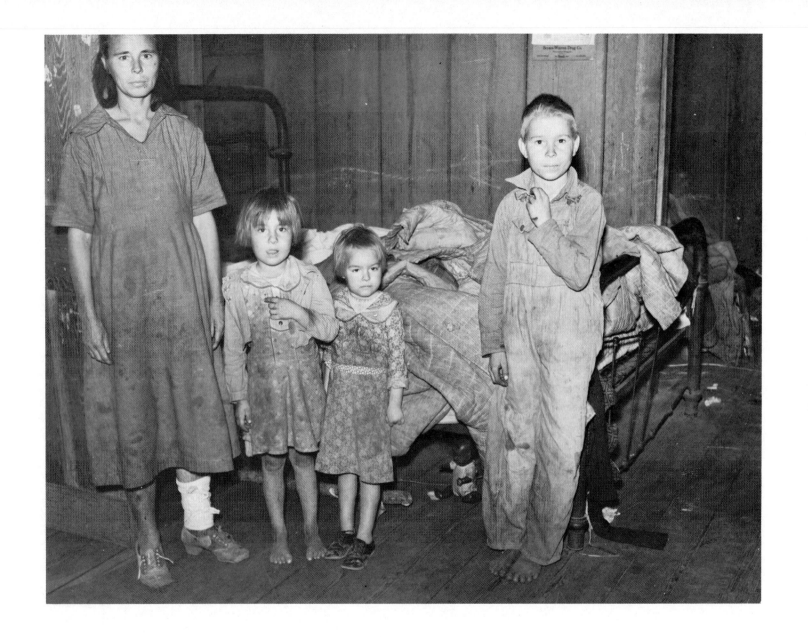

A treadle-operated sewing machine was a prize possession on any farm, whether used to make quilts for sale or for general sewing. Newspapers on cabin walls were effective and inexpensive insulation material, but the contrast between the cabin occupants' lives and the images presented in the ads is striking. Both photographs were made at Farm Security Administration projects. The photo on this page, at Gee's Bend in 1937, and that on the facing page, at Skyline Farms near Scottsboro in 1935, were made by Arthur Rothstein. (Library of Congress)

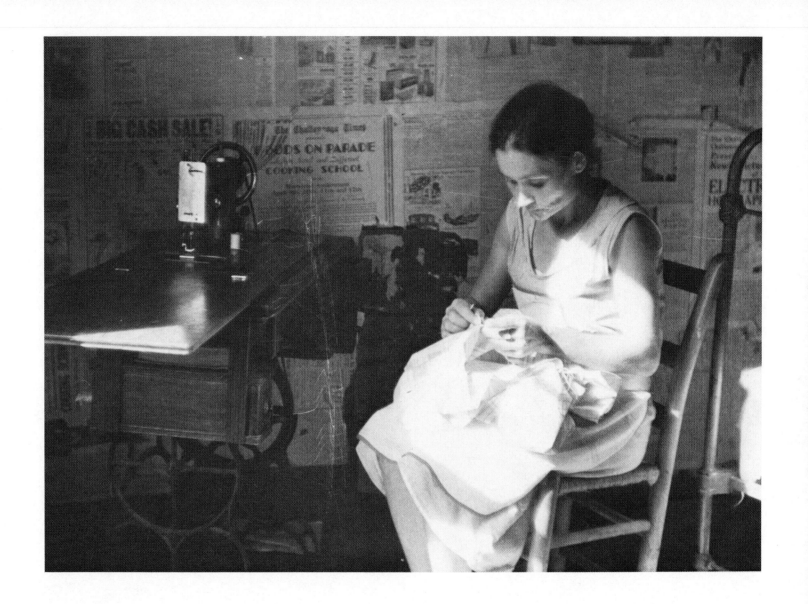

In large families even the young children were expected to do their share of the chores while older family members worked in the fields planting, hoeing, and harvesting the crop. Arthur Rothstein made this photo of such a family at Gee's Bend in 1937. (Library of Congress)

Most farmers did not get into town very often. When they did, it was a special day for the family. These farm folk, who came into Eden, Alabama, for a day in 1936, were photographed by Dorothea Lange. (Library of Congress)

For most rural people the general store was the source of supplies they had to have but could not produce for themselves. Traditionally, the store was owned by the same person who owned the land they farmed. Debts to the merchant/landowner assured the inescapable and enduring dependency of the tenant farmer. Efforts to break this pattern included the establishment of farmers' cooperative stores such as this one at Gee's Bend owned by the farmers themselves. Marion Post Wolcott photograph. (Library of Congress)

In Moundville, Walker Evans recorded the tempo of small-town life and the effects of the depression on food prices. For those few with money, three pounds of potatoes for a dime was a good deal. But for Alabama's farmers the collapse of the prices paid for their crop was disastrous. (Library of Congress)

While on assignment for the Farm Security Administration, Dorothea Lange made a photograph that captured the depths of poverty and the slow pace of life in the small towns of Alabama. In this picture, made in Eden, the ox wagon contrasts sharply with the billboard in the background advertising the latest V-8 Ford. Such visual contrasts often enliven FSA photographs. (Library of Congress)

Outside the Black Belt, specifically in south Alabama's Wiregrass region, agricultural diversification, which began after the boll weevil's devastating attacks, cushioned the depression's blow. In this 1936 picture of Florala's Masonic parade, which has been held every June since antebellum times, the town and its people are lively and prosperous. (Florala Public Library)

Even Progressive Governor Bibb Graves, shown at his desk during his 1927–31 term, was overwhelmed by the depression's impact on the state's revenue and thus on its ability to deal with the crisis. While most state politicians, including Graves's successor, Governor "Plain Bill" Brandon, counseled retrenchment and a balanced budget, President Franklin Roosevelt would offer the country a "New Deal." (Alabama Department of Archives and History)

Alabama's rescue from the clutches of the depression would depend far more on FDR and his policies than on those of state or local governments, private business initiatives, or charities. Shortly after his victory over Herbert Hoover, the president-elect traveled to Muscle Shoals to inspect the Wilson Dam and the nitrate plants that would become important elements in the Tennessee Valley Authority. In this photo Roosevelt greeted elected officials from Alabama and Tennessee on his arrival at Sheffield, January 23, 1932. (Birmingham Public Library, Archives and Manuscripts)

On May 18, 1933, President Roosevelt returned to Muscle Shoals to sign the historic Morris-Hill bill creating the Tennessee Valley Authority. The resulting construction projects brought an immediate flood of jobs, and the long-term benefits in improved navigation and abundant electrical power would transform a chronically depressed portion of the state into one of its most prosperous regions. (Alabama Department of Archives and History)

Construction progressed rapidly on projects throughout the Tennessee River Valley, including the Wheeler Dam, fifteen miles above the Wilson Dam and shown in this photograph made in December 1935. The dam was begun in November 1933 and completed in October 1936 at a cost of more than $42 million. When this photograph was made, nearly 5,000 men were employed on the project. (Birmingham Public Library, Archives and Manuscripts)

12-6-35-WH-11,972

It is hardly surprising that in no part of the United States was FDR more popular than in Alabama, especially in the Tennessee Valley. His re-election in 1936 in a national landslide victory over Alf Landon was celebrated in Florence with a mock burial of the Republican challenger, while men carried signs associating Roosevelt and the TVA with progress, prosperity, and democratic government. G. W. Landrum photograph. (Jerry Landrum, Florence)

Important as it was in north Alabama, TVA was only one of several New Deal agencies that operated in the state. The Civilian Conservation Corps had many camps around Alabama, including one in the Talladega National Forest where these men were employed making roofing shingles in 1933. (Birmingham Public Library, Archives and Manuscripts)

Throughout the state various agencies undertook public works projects; the WPA is the best-remembered of them all. Not only did it construct many worthwhile public projects, it also provided employment to Alabamians in all walks of life, from construction workers to artists, actors, and writers. This photograph shows an early road job near Greensboro. (Library of Congress)

In Mobile the WPA put men to work clearing malaria-infected Three Mile Creek, which bounded the city on its north side. Such labor-intensive projects were typical of the WPA approach. (University of South Alabama Photographic Archives)

The Farm Security Administration operated in many Alabama counties. Its diverse activities included a rural rehabilitation program that supported traveling home economists whose job was to raise the standard of farm life through practical education. In these 1939 photographs by Marion Post Wolcott, FSA home economists visit clients in Coffee (this page) and Pike (facing page) counties. Charged with documenting the agency's work, FSA photographers, under the direction of Roy Stryker, amassed a priceless portrait of the depression. They took hundreds of pictures throughout Alabama alone. (Library of Congress)

Many people were willing to try almost anything to survive the depression's hard times. F. M. Pointer, "The Old Reliable House Mover," also was selling fish, fruits, and vegetables in his roadside stand near Birmingham when Walker Evans made this picture in 1936. (Library of Congress)

The hungry years of the depression found many Alabamians "putting up" fruits, vegetables, and preserves whenever they could. The federal government and the Cooperative Extension Service taught proper home-canning methods. The well-stocked pantry kept by this mother and daughter reflected the success of their programs. This photograph was made in Coffee County in 1939 by Marion Post Wolcott. (Library of Congress)

In the midst of poverty and ignorance many Alabamians turned to education in hopes of bettering their lot. In this school and church at Gee's Bend, classes were taught for adults and children. The academic level of the instruction was undoubtedly modest and the building was dilapidated, because public funding for the education of rural black Alabamians was virtually nonexistent. Arthur Rothstein made this photo in 1937 as children left school at the end of the day. (Library of Congress)

174

Despite the reform efforts in the 1920s, the quality of Alabama's rural schools tended to perpetuate high rates of illiteracy and ignorance among both blacks and whites. This photograph, made in 1939 by Marion Post Wolcott, shows one of the classes that were conducted with federal funds in an effort to reduce adult illiteracy. (Library of Congress)

Children who lived in the countryside were unlikely to have decent schools to attend. These barefoot boys, sitting on rough-hewn home-made chairs, are attending a reading class that was held out of doors in the sandy school yard. The photograph was made by Carl Mydans at the Cumberland Mountain Farms near Scottsboro in June 1936. (Library of Congress)

In February 1937 it was too cold to have school out of doors at the Skyline Farms project near Scottsboro when Arthur Rothstein made this picture of a class sitting around an oil-drum stove. The physical facilities were spartan, and teachers in the rural Tennessee Valley were paid less than half the salary of their Birmingham counterparts. (Library of Congress)

177

With better funding, the urban Alabama schools undertook more than the "three R's." In this photo Birmingham schoolchildren prepare for a cooking demonstration at Norwood School in the early 1930s. (Birmingham Public Library, Archives and Manuscripts)

In November 1930, as the
depression worsened, these
Birmingham children lined up
for soup at their school
lunchroom. For many youngsters, the food the school
supplied was probably the
most nourishing meal they
got all day. (Birmingham
Public Library, Archives and
Manuscripts)

The children in most urban schools enjoyed educational opportunities far superior to those in rural parts of Alabama. Teachers in Birmingham were among the best paid in the state as the city prided itself on its support for public education. Too few Alabama classrooms were as nicely equipped as this one in a north Birmingham school, which was photographed in 1930. (Birmingham Public Library, Archives and Manuscripts)

In the 1920s Mobile constructed a new school complex that became Murphy High School. Known for its high academic standards, Murphy educated the offspring of a broad cross section of the city's white population. The scholars in this photo are working in the boys' study hall. Erik Overbey photograph. (University of South Alabama Photographic Archives)

Urban Alabama's children had extracurricular activities that ranged from listening to FDR speak to the nation on a radio lent to the Eleventh Street School in Gadsden especially for that purpose, to membership in organizations such as the Cathedral School Girls Band in Mobile. Urban institutions, public, private or parochial, were far more likely to offer children such opportunities than their poorer rural counterparts. Left photograph by Albert Lebourg. (Frank Lebourg, Gadsden) Right photograph by Erik Overbey. (University of South Alabama Photographic Archives)

Segregation and depression economics severely limited educational opportunities for black Alabamians. Urban areas provided blacks the best chance for high school education, usually at vocationally oriented schools. These students at Birmingham Industrial High School were learning to be cobblers in this 1930 photograph. Throughout the interwar years funding for black education was woefully inadequate, with black teachers being paid less than one-third as much as their white counterparts. (Birmingham Public Library, Archives and Manuscripts)

Black children who attended the Mobile County Training School learned a variety of trades, such as mattress making and carpentry. But the school also stressed academic subjects and produced many of the leaders of Mobile's black community in this century. Blacks throughout Alabama took pride in the achievements of their children and the dedication of their teachers but were powerless to increase the financial support their public schools received. S. Blake McNeely photograph. (University of South Alabama Photographic Archives)

For those fortunate enough to continue their education beyond high school, extracurricular activities always have been one of the principal attractions of going to college. Auburn certainly was no exception. Coeds (this page) show the boys basic cooking techniques at a "Sadie Hawkins Day" party, while entering freshmen (facing page) are entertained at a dance welcoming them to Auburn. (Auburn University Archives)

Whether black or white, Alabama colleges had their cheerleaders, and the major schools had football teams. The photo on this page shows the spirited Tuskegee cheerleading squad. (Tuskegee Institute Archives) On the facing page, the University of Alabama tangles with Vanderbilt on October 25, 1930, at Legion Field in Birmingham. Alabama won the game, 12–7. (The University of Alabama, Special Collections)

Alabamians' love of football extended to all-star games as well. These young men are participating in the festivities in downtown Montgomery prior to the 1940 Blue–Gray game. (Alabama Department of Archives and History)

Although no other college sport challenged football's popularity, boxing more than matched its brutality. Here George Corley Wallace, boxing for the University of Alabama, batters his bloodied Tulane rival in a 1939 match. (The University of Alabama, Special Collections)

Many Alabamians followed college athletic events, but few were college graduates. For most people education beyond the "three R's" was a luxury that could be justified only if it helped in getting a job. The men in the 1930 photo on this page are studying textile math in a night class in Birmingham's Avondale Mill School. (Birmingham Public Library, Archives and Manuscripts) On the facing page, a young woman learns to take dictation at the city's Alverson Business School, ca. 1934. Fred A. Powell photograph. (Jackie Dobbs, Old Birmingham Photographs)

Public libraries were popular in the depression as a means of both self-improvement and inexpensive recreation. The Gadsden Public Library's children's room, shown in this 1938 photo, offered its patrons access to the wider world of literature and the arts. New library buildings were constructed in several cities, including Mobile and Birmingham, during the 1920s. However, funding for libraries as well as schools suffered as the depression reduced local tax collection. (Birmingham Public Library, Archives and Manuscripts)

In another approach to self-improvement and recreation, Tuskegee Institute sponsored training programs for Boy Scouts. In this 1932 photograph young black scouts practice a first-aid drill. (Tuskegee Institute Archives)

Recreation for most of Alabama's rural population included music and square dancing, which were part of a way of life and a relief from the hardships of the depression. In these photographs Ben Shahn captured musicians and dancers at the Farm Security Administration's Skyline Farms project near Scottsboro in 1937. (Library of Congress)

In Alabama's cities cooking demonstrations, often sponsored by the local gas and electric utilities, which charged no admission fee, were popular during the 1930s. The audience filled the Birmingham Municipal Auditorium to capacity when this picture was made. (Birmingham Public Library, Archives and Manuscripts)

The depression saw elaborate amateur theatrical productions that enabled actors and audiences to escape the harsh realities of daily life. This 1934 photo shows a dramatic scene from "The American Plan," a production that featured several prominent Birmingham citizens. (Birmingham Public Library, Archives and Manuscripts)

During the 1930s, radio became part of everyday life in the state's metropolitan areas. Local "personalities" emerged, often as band leaders, such as WAPI's "Happy Hal" Byrnes, shown in this O. V. Hunt photograph. (Birmingham Public Library, Archives and Manuscripts)

WODX ("Where Old Dixie Xports") had just started broadcasting from the Battle House in Mobile when Erik Overbey made this picture. The studio band, under the direction of Al Treadway and with Eddie King at the piano, played requests every Saturday night. By the end of the decade, Alabama's radio stations, with their local celebrities and network connections, had become an increasingly important source of up-to-the-minute news and information and inexpensive entertainment. (University of South Alabama Photographic Archives)

For many urban Alabamians a trip to the country, even for a picnic, was a welcome diversion. The 1933 Catanzano Brothers' picnic was enlivened by a spirit that was not yet quite legal. Although Alabamians generally supported the "Noble Experiment" in public, whatever their private inclinations, most Americans had had enough and voted to repeal Prohibition in that year. O. V. Hunt photograph. (Birmingham Public Library, Archives and Manuscripts)

Alabamians showed considerable ingenuity in overcoming depression-era obstacles to family vacations. To beat the high cost of tourist accommodations, the Lebourg family of Gadsden used a homemade pop-up camper for their outings in 1937. It would be years before such vehicles were built commercially. Albert Lebourg photograph. (Frank Lebourg, Gadsden)

Like most Americans, Alabamians were fascinated by automobile and motorcycle races. The contests in these photographs occurred in Gadsden. Despite the danger of vehicles catching fire or hitting spectators, the crowd stood close to the track as locals competed with one another and against drivers from other areas. Albert Lebourg photographs. (Frank Lebourg, Gadsden)

Indeed, no society has ever been so closely identified with the automobile as has the United States. In this photograph, made in Birmingham in 1936, the billboard's message contrasts sharply with the squalid buildings and vacant lot that surround it. (Library of Congress)

A more optimistic note was struck when the Birmingham Municipal Auditorium played host to an automobile show presented by General Motors in the late 1930s. By the end of the decade, the prosperity the new cars symbolized had begun to return to Alabama and the nation. (Birmingham Public Library, Archives and Manuscripts)

A trip up Red Mountain to visit the new location of the statue of Vulcan was a pleasant outing. The WPA had moved the god of the forge from the fairgrounds to a pedestal in the midst of a park on the mountain overlooking Birmingham. But even without Vulcan, the fairgrounds, shown on the facing page, still had its midway, which gleamed with the alluring delights of ferris wheels, bumper cars, and other wild, big-city rides. Vulcan photograph by Albert Lebourg. (Frank Lebourg, Gadsden; fairgrounds photograph, Birmingham Public Library, Archives and Manuscripts)

Even in the worst days of the depression, Mardi Gras continued to offer Mobilians an escape from the cares of everyday life into the realm of King Felix. Each year elaborate floats with costumed knights and ladies paraded around Bienville Square, and the depression saw some of the most beautiful floats ever constructed for the carnival. Erik Overbey made this photograph on Mardi Gras day in 1933. (University of South Alabama Photographic Archives)

During the Mardi Gras season, balls were given by various Mystic societies. Invitations to these events were much sought after, for, unlike the parades, they were not open to the public. Pictured here is the 1938 Infant Mystic's ball at the Battle House. S. Blake McNeely photograph. (University of South Alabama Photographic Archives)

"Bill Pipes" and His Melody Barons.

Mobilians were not the only urbanites dancing. Swing music, or the Big Band sound, was popular in all the state's cities and towns by the end of the decade. This music cut across racial lines to entertain audiences with tunes by groups like Bill Pipes and the "Tuskegee Melody Barons" or Bobby Adams's "Auburn Knights." (Left photograph, Tuskegee Institute Archives; right photograph, Huntsville–Madison County Public Library)

213

Although times were getting better for many Alabamians by the end of the thirties, progress was uneven. The couple in the 1937 photograph on this page are relaxing in the comfortable living room of their new home at Bankhead Farms, a Farm Security Administration project in Birmingham. Birmingham's economy rebounded from the depression more rapidly than Mobile's, and it had received far more direct federal assistance. By contrast, John Gaston's modest hand-lettered sign, the unpainted houses on his street, and the weary men walking along the sidewalk suggest that in April 1937 good times still lay in the future for many Mobilians. Arthur Rothstein photographs. (Library of Congress)

Mobile's port long had provided employment for many of the city's black males. But, whether opening oysters by the thousands, stevedoring, or breaking up scrap metal, the jobs had been scarce and the pay low. In the late 1930s, however, business was beginning to revive, especially in the port's scrap metal yards, and the employment picture brightened. Left photograph by Erik Overbey; right photograph by S. Blake McNeely. (University of South Alabama Photographic Archives)

From 1937 until weeks before the attack on Pearl Harbor, tons of scrap metal left Mobile, bound for ports in Japan and Germany. Attracted by the chance to turn rusting junk into cash, Alabamians brought scrap to the waterfront in cars, some of which were in little better condition than their contents. S. Blake McNeely photograph. (University of South Alabama Photographic Archives)

Business was brisk as mounds of scrap that had been collected from industry and private citizens waited to be loaded on outbound ships, many of which flew the flags of nations the United States soon would be fighting in World War II. S. Blake McNeely photograph. (University of South Alabama Photographic Archives)

As the United States began to rearm in the years before the attack on Pearl Harbor, orders for Birmingham iron, steel, and coal increased dramatically. The photo on this page, made in 1939 by Fred A. Powell, shows the Sloss-Sheffield works. (Jackie Dobbs, Old Birmingham Photographs) The photo on the facing page, taken in 1939 by Roy Carter, Sr., shows miners digging coal at Parrish, Alabama. (*Birmingham News*)

Defense-related production brought industrial expansion and new jobs throughout Alabama. In this photo, men are making boots and shoes for military contracts at the General Shoe Company in Huntsville. (Huntsville–Madison County Public Library)

In 1939 the *Birmingham News* undertook a survey of reviving industrial activity in the region. This photograph, which was made in Anniston as workers poured molten iron into pipe molds, was part of that project. Roy Carter, Sr., photograph. (*Birmingham News*)

In 1939 the Goodyear Tire
and Rubber Company held
important defense contracts
but also worked to produce
tires for the growing civilian
demand spurred by the return
of prosperity. Whether in-
specting and balancing tires
or mixing the batches of rubber, there was work once
again in Gadsden. Roy
Carter, Sr., photographs.
(*Birmingham News*)

225

The war would bring drastic changes to life in Alabama. The sleepy town of Childersburg (population 400), whose pace of life is suggested by this photograph, was turned upside down by the opening of a $70 million DuPont munitions plant and the sudden surge in population its jobs attracted. Jack Delano photograph. (Library of Congress)

The man in this photo by Jack Delano looks at a list of jobs available "At Once," though five years earlier he would have found little or nothing. The wartime boom was not limited to Childersburg; several other towns and cities across the state had similar experiences. (Library of Congress)

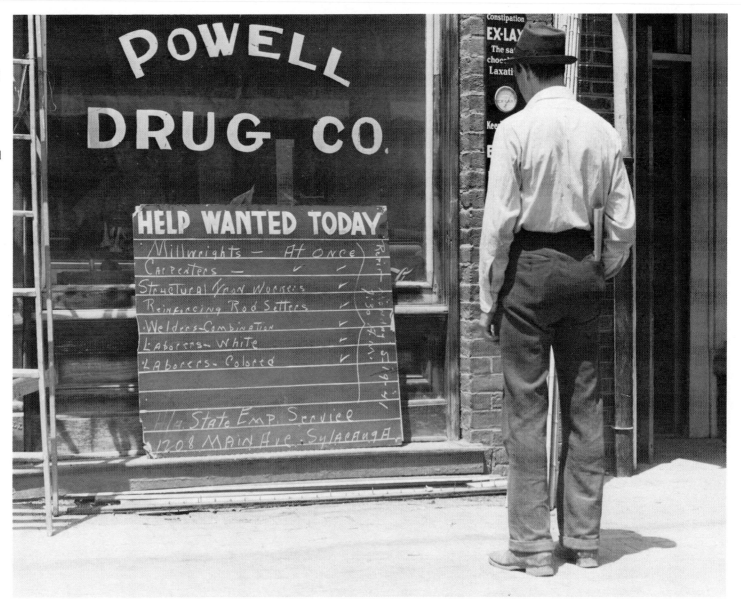

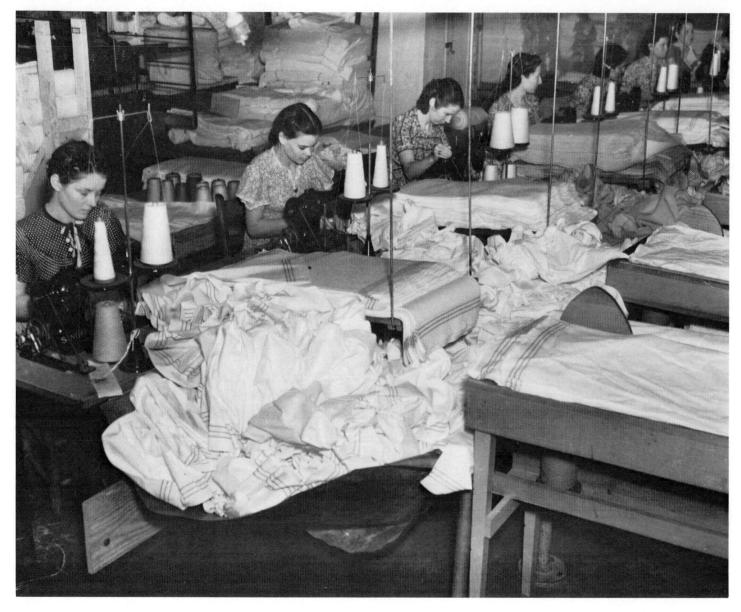

Although women had worked in textile mills in the South since the nineteenth century, the eve of war saw the number of such jobs increase dramatically. In the photo on this page, made by Roy Carter, Sr., female employees hem towels at the Fairfax Mills. (*Birmingham News*) On the facing page, women work the looms in the Huntsville Manufacturing Company. (Huntsville–Madison County Public Library) In addition to increasing the number of jobs, the war also greatly expanded the range of employment opportunities.

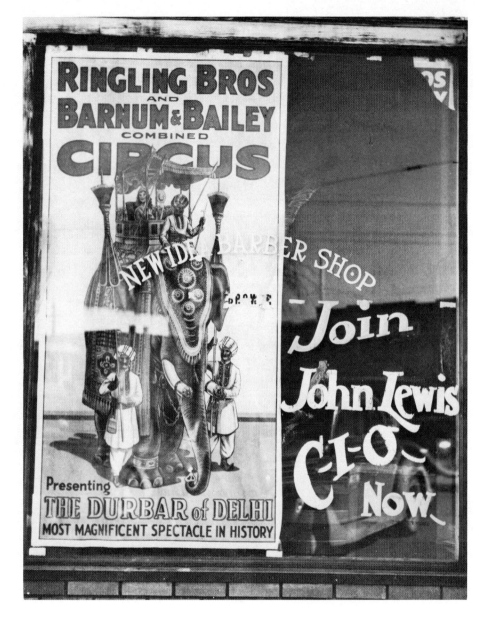

Outside the textile mills, the New Deal had effected a dramatic change in the climate for organized labor. In Birmingham in the thirties and in Mobile during World War II, the Congress of Industrial Organizations succeeded where unionization previously had failed. It organized unskilled and semiskilled workers in large numbers. The Arthur Rothstein photo of the barber shop window exhorting patrons to join the CIO was made in Birmingham in 1936. (Library of Congress)

This photo of a CIO meeting was made in Mobile during World War II as the union was organizing the thousands of new shipyard workers. Although Alabama's oldest trade union had been formed by printers in the Port City in antebellum times, the CIO was a radical departure from such craft unions in size and style. Erik Overbey photograph. (University of South Alabama Photographic Archives)

As the United States moved closer to entering the world war, industrial relations in Birmingham still were marred by bitter disputes. The photo on this page shows men trying to convince a carload of workers not to cross their picket line in a 1941 strike at TCI's Ensley steel mill. On the facing page, armed company guards line up for inspection during the strike. The weapon held by the guard in the foreground is probably a tear-gas launcher. Roy Carter, Sr., photographs. (*Birmingham News*)

233

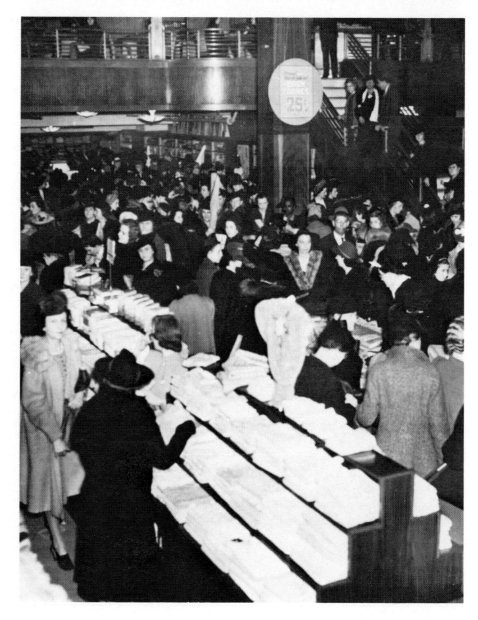

Labor difficulties notwith-
standing, Alabamians had
money to spend in the early
forties and retail sales rebounded. In the spring of
1940, Loveman's Department
Store in Birmingham was
mobbed during its annual
twenty-five-cents sale. (Birmingham Public Library, Archives and Manuscripts)

In Mobile, Hammel's Department Store featured decorations honoring Walt Disney's *Pinocchio* in its extravagant 1940 Christmas promotion. Prosperity had returned and war workers already were flooding the city, filling jobs in shipyards and on federal construction projects. Erik Overbey photograph. (University of South Alabama Photographic Archives)

235

In the face of the darkening international scene, Alabamians retained a lively appreciation of their history and heritage. Monte Sano had been acquired by the state of Alabama and made over into a public park by Civilian Conservation Corps workers in the late thirties. The park opened on August 25, 1938. Among the dignitaries present was William Bankhead, Speaker of the United States House of Representatives, who is at the podium in this picture. (Huntsville–Madison County Public Library)

During the following year's celebration at Monte Sano, citizens staged a historical pageant that was set in Huntsville during the Civil War. Its last performance was on September 1, 1939, the day Hitler invaded Poland, beginning World War II in Europe. (Huntsville–Madison County Public Library)

In December 1940 the supervisors of the TCI Ensley works gathered for a formal picture with a traditional Christmas scene in the background. A year later, two weeks after the Japanese attack on Pearl Harbor, the Christmas greenery was gone, replaced by a sign which proclaimed that the mill was now a defense plant, part of the "Arsenal of Democracy." The United States had gone to war. (Birmingham Public Library, Archives and Manuscripts)

On the eve of war Alabama remained a land of sharp contrasts. In Birmingham and other cities regular passenger air service was available, while in rural counties many people still depended upon mule-drawn wagons. However, many Alabamians had left the land, never to return, and of those who remained many more would leave for better-paying jobs in war industries. The mule-drawn wagon's day was nearly done. In the Albert Lebourg photograph on this page, a Delta airliner arrives at Birmingham's Municipal Airport. (Frank Lebourg, Gadsden) In the S. Blake McNeely photograph on the facing page, a farmer in Baldwin County brings his potato crop to market. (University of South Alabama Photographic Archives)

Military parades, such as the one shown on this page, photographed during a war bond rally in Mobile in 1943, were important in keeping spirits up on the home front during the war. High morale was essential to production of war matériel, Alabama's principal contribution to the war effort in addition to thousands of the state's men and women serving in the armed forces. Thousands more, including the shipyard worker shown in the photo on the facing page, took jobs in defense-related industries. (University of South Alabama Photographic Archives)

In addition to virtually eliminating unemployment, the war brought a dramatic increase in job opportunities for blacks and women in Alabama. Pressured by the NAACP, the federal government eventually required nondiscriminatory hiring by all defense contractors. With the expansion of industry and the draft, the civilian labor pool was adequate only if women were hired to do jobs that formerly had been held by men. By 1943 women and blacks were working in the widest variety of jobs at the highest rates of pay they had ever received. In this photograph a young furnace operator pauses at his job at Muscle Shoals Nitrate Plant #2 in 1943. Billy Glenn photograph. (Tennessee Valley Authority, National Fertilizer Development Center)

At the Birmingham Electric Company, operators of the city's bus lines, a woman pumps diesel fuel while the vehicle is serviced at the city bus barn in 1943. (Birmingham Public Library, Archives and Manuscripts)

Forty thousand men and women worked in Mobile's shipyards, and the Alabama Dry Dock and Shipbuilding Company was the city's largest employer during World War II. In this photo some of ADDSCO's employees are leaving the yard at the afternoon shift change. (University of South Alabama Photographic Archives)

ADDSCO expanded rapidly after 1939 in response to increased defense spending. By the end of World War II, the yard had built 122 ships and repaired or refitted more than 2,800 others. In this wartime photo the skyline of Mobile is barely visible beyond the sea of ships berthed at ADDSCO. (University of South Alabama Photographic Archives)

Mobile's three major ship-yards built an average of one ship a week by working around the clock during the war. Many of the jobs were dangerous. As an example, in this 1943 photo men prepared the tumble blocks under a ship's hull prior to its launching. (University of South Alabama Photographic Archives)

The shipyards also used a variety of heavy machinery, such as this pneumatic hammer. The picture is unusual because work crews generally were segregated. In a second picture of this scene made at the time, the black man was excluded. (University of South Alabama Photographic Archives)

Because the shipyards grew so fast, most new employees had to be trained to do their jobs. This was especially true of women and blacks doing skilled industrial work. In the photo on this page ADDSCO's first female instructor shows a student how to use a welding torch, while in the picture on the facing page a black welder learns his trade. Resentment against black welders resulted in a two-day race riot at ADDSCO in May 1943, but blacks continued to be employed in skilled positions by defense contractors throughout Alabama. (University of South Alabama Photographic Archives)

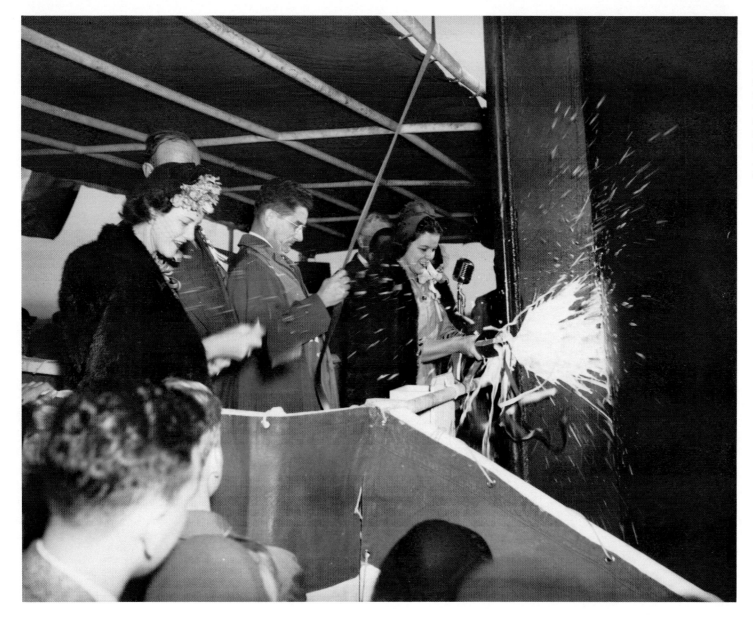

During the war many women continued to play traditional roles, including the young woman doing the honors at the launching of the SS *Joel Chandler Harris* at ADDSCO in 1942. (University of South Alabama Photographic Archives)

Physical handicaps were no barrier to participation in the war effort, as these blind seamstresses in Talladega demonstrated. They were sewing pillowcases for use by the armed forces. (Auburn University Archives)

Women who worked in industrial establishments in Alabama earned far more money than those who held teaching and clerical jobs. As a result, there was a critical shortage of teachers, saleswomen, and office workers, especially in areas with large defense plants. In the Billy Glenn photo on this page, a woman operates an overhead crane at Muscle Shoals Nitrate Plant #2. (Tennessee Valley Authority, National Fertilizer Development Center) On the facing page, women work on an ammunition line in the Redstone Ordnance Plant. (Redstone Arsenal, Huntsville)

254

World War II changed the
lives of a generation of
American college students.
On this page, young men at
Auburn register for the draft
during 1941. On the facing
page, subdued young people
at Auburn listen via loud-
speakers as Congress declares
war on December 8, 1941.
(Auburn University Archives)

Reserve Officers' Training Corps units filled rapidly at Alabama's universities and colleges. In the 1943 photo on this page, University of Alabama cadets parade past the Denny Chimes. (The University of Alabama, Special Collections) On the facing page, cadets at Tuskegee Institute pose in front of Booker T. Washington's statue in a 1942 photo by Arthur Rothstein. (Library of Congress) Throughout World War II, the regular armed forces and ROTC continued to be segregated.

Many Allied pilots received their flight training at bases in Alabama during the war. In this photo one student pilot describes his experiences to another as they train at Montgomery's Gunter Field. Twelve thousand pilots went through basic flight school at Gunter during the war. (Maxwell Air Force Base, Air University Office of History)

Students sometimes got unexpected visits from celebrities. For example, Jack Dempsey, heavyweight boxing champion, is shown as he visited Royal Air Force pilots training at Gunter Field. (Alabama Department of Archives and History)

In a precedent-shattering decision, the army bowed to NAACP pressure and began training black pilots at Tuskegee in 1941. In this photo, three cadets meet with their instructor beside their trainers at the newly completed Moton Field. (Maxwell Air Force Base, Air University Office of History)

In addition to flying instruction, cadets studied aircraft armament as part of their training. The first black pilots served in the famed Ninety-ninth Pursuit Squadron, which later became part of the 332nd Fighter Group. The unit built an admirable military reputation, flying 1,600 combat missions across Europe by the war's end. (Maxwell Air Force Base, Air University Office of History)

Besides doubling its civilian population, wartime Mobile was also temporary home for thousands of men serving in the crews of Allied ships being refitted, overhauled, or repaired in the city's ship-yards. Recreation facilities for ship crews, such as this one photographed by Erik Over-bey in 1944, were woefully inadequate. (University of South Alabama Photographic Archives)

All large employers provided some recreation for their workers, including frequent bond rallies. At a rally in 1944, the ADDSCO band plays for an impromptu dance contest. (University of South Alabama Photographic Archives)

At the same 1944 rally, workers held a mock lynching of General Tojo, the hated Japanese warlord. His gasoline-soaked effigy was hanged and burned in a process chillingly reminiscent of the hundreds of real lynchings that had occurred in Alabama and the South since Reconstruction. At least two of these mock lynchings were held so that the shipyard workers on other shifts also could participate. (University of South Alabama Photographic Archives)

267

The home front was an important target for wartime propaganda, including posters urging shipyard workers who were waiting to "clock in" to seek treatment for venereal disease, which reached near-epidemic proportions in wartime Mobile. (University of South Alabama Photographic Archives)

Aided by schoolchildren, students at Auburn collected aluminum for defense purposes in 1942. Such drives were as important for their impact on civilian morale as for the metal collected. (Auburn University Archives)

Whether under military orders or traveling to war-industry towns where the jobs were, people were on the move throughout Alabama during the war. The soldiers pictured here at Union Station in Montgomery were getting directions from civilian USO volunteers in 1944. (Alabama Department of Archives and History)

The family in this 1940 photograph by Erik Overbey was living in a trailer camp on the eastern shore of Mobile Bay, having come for jobs in shipyards or at Brookley Field. Although life in a trailer was far from ideal, the wages more than made up for the hardships. Many of the state's war workers had never had jobs as good as those available to them during the conflict. (University of South Alabama Photographic Archives)

Because of the rapid influx of workers housing was inadequate in war-industry cities such as Mobile. The men in this 1943 photograph were at a War Housing Center trying to get in one of the housing projects the federal government had built in and around the city. (University of South Alabama Photographic Archives)

Those who did manage to get into housing projects such as the one on Blakely Island were a fortunate minority. Other workers spent the war in tents, trailers, converted warehouses, or shantytowns. Blacks had the greatest difficulty because only two of the area's sixteen federal housing projects were open to them. (University of South Alabama Photographic Archives)

Childersburg's dramatic growth after the DuPont plant's construction there also caused severe housing shortages. The tent camp in the 1941 photo by Jack Delano was for white workers while "My Bunk House" in the 1942 photo by John Collier was for blacks. (Library of Congress)

274

In the Tennessee Valley, Ingalls Shipbuilding Company in Decatur constructed ocean-going barges on the Tennessee River. The Ingalls facility, like shipyards in Mobile, worked around the clock throughout the war. Jack Delano made this photo in 1942. (Library of Congress)

The abundant electric power provided by TVA was used by a variety of defense industries. This photo made at the Reynolds Metals plant in Sheffield in 1942 shows the foreman of the hot mill. The heroic pose and dramatic lighting in this photograph suggest its eventual use as propaganda. In fact, it was one of a series on the daily life of this man and his family made for the Office of War Information by Jack Delano. (Library of Congress)

With so many women working in war jobs, child care was a major problem. Schools were on double shifts and preschoolers often had no place to go. Women such as these ADDSCO welders generally had to rely on friends and neighbors to watch their children. (University of South Alabama Photographic Archives)

A lucky few found places for their children in one of the federally funded day-care facilities that were established for war workers. However, there were many more children than places available in facilities such as this one in Mobile. (University of South Alabama Photographic Archives)

Many entertainers visited Alabama's military installations and defense industries to help boost morale or sell war bonds. Sometimes the visitor was not only famous but also a native Alabamian. In this Ed Jones photo, Tallulah Bankhead had returned home to Jasper for a visit and bond rally. (*Birmingham News*)

Not all the entertainers were as famous as Tallulah. On November 11, 1944, Armistice Day, a group of midgets held a bond rally at ADDSCO. Alabamians led the nation in the sale of war bonds. (University of South Alabama Photographic Archives)

With training facilities scattered across the state, thousands of servicemen and women were stationed in Alabama during the war. One of the most popular amusements for off-duty personnel was a USO dance or sing-a-long. The photograph on this page shows a Montgomery dance. (Alabama Department of Archives and History) The photograph on the facing page shows a sing-a-long at the Birmingham USO headquarters. (Birmingham Public Library, Archives and Manuscripts) USO centers existed throughout Alabama, catering to both blacks and whites.

Exhibits of military hardware drew large civilian crowds whenever they were set up. In the photo on this page, sober-faced workers in Mobile surround a machine gun display. (University of South Alabama Photographic Archives) On the facing page, people crowd past an "Airborne Exhibit," which was part of a special train that came through Anniston in December 1945 to promote Victory Bond sales. (Anniston–Calhoun County Public Library)

In addition to military exhibits, the Victory Bond campaign also offered people a chance to win household appliances that had been otherwise unavailable "for the duration." Thanks to wartime high wages and steady employment, Alabama's workers had more money than they had ever dreamed of a few years earlier, but there was little to buy with the cash until after the war. (Anniston–Calhoun County Public Library)

When the Victory Bond drawing was held, a blind-folded youngster picked out the winner's ticket for the new refrigerator behind her. The prize made quite a Christmas present, for the event was held in Anniston on December 22, 1945. (Anniston–Calhoun County Public Library)

"Hurry up and wait" was a phrase well known to every wartime serviceman and merchant mariner. In this 1945 photograph, men kill time shooting pool while their ships are in a Mobile dry dock. (University of South Alabama Photographic Archives)

On May 20, 1945, shipyard workers crowded into the main yard at ADDSCO to celebrate V-E Day. Although many ships were being refitted and overhauled for the war in the Pacific, workers were being laid off in the spring and summer as rapidly as they had been hired in 1940. (University of South Alabama Photographic Archives)

On August 15, 1945, V-J
Day, World War II ended. In
Huntsville, D. C. Monroe
and his band gave a concert
on the steps of the courthouse and a crowd filled the
square to enjoy the music.
Traditional celebrations such
as this were held in towns
across Alabama as the second
world war in a generation
came to an end. (H. E.
Monroe, Huntsville)

In Birmingham, V-J Day was the occasion for a night of celebration and impromptu street parties. Girls hugged soldiers they had never met, children stayed up late, and some young people decorated their Plymouth with a last effigy of the despised Tojo. Their play on words, "I got the atomic ache," has lost some of its humor over the years. Prosperous beyond their wildest depression-era dreams, Alabamians confidently faced a future whose challenges to their way of life they perceived about as clearly as these students understood the implications of the dawn of the Atomic Age. Photographs by Roy Carter, Sr. (left), and Neal Sheridan (right). (*Birmingham News*)

Annotated Bibliography
of Photographic Sources

Alabama Department of Archives and History, Montgomery
The wide-ranging photographic collection touches on virtually any topic. The Mrs. J. L. Prentiss Collection in the Manuscripts Division has material on United Service Organizations (USO) activities in World War II.

Anniston–Calhoun County Public Library
The local history and genealogy section contains a good collection of local photographs made throughout the period under study.

Auburn University Archives
The photographs of the Cooperative Extension Service provide an excellent view of rural life as well as an unusually vivid picture of campus life on the eve of World War II.

Bessemer Hall of History Museum
This diverse collection includes several excellent photographs of economic activity and one of a KKK rally in Bessemer.

Birmingham News Reference Library
The *Birmingham News* has the best collection of photographs in the state outside the major archives. This is an outstanding source for pictures from the mid-1930s forward. It is not generally open to the public because its staff and facilities are busy serving the daily needs of the newspaper.

Birmingham Public Library, Department of Archives and Manuscripts
Photographs by O. V. Hunt, the Birmingham View Company, and an excellent selection of Farm Security Administration prints are the highlights of this outstanding collection, which also is well organized.

Jackie Dobbs Collection, Birmingham
The Dobbs Collection contains Old Birmingham photographs made by the Birmingham View Company throughout the first half of this century.

Florala Public Library
The library has several views of the 1936 Masonic parade, among other items of local interest.

Huntsville–Madison County Public Library
An excellent regional collection of photographs especially valuable for the economic and social historian exists in the Henry B. Zeitler Room at the library.

Jerry Landrum Collection, Florence
The interesting photographs by G. W. Landrum, a commercial photographer in Florence for many years, are available from his son.

Frank Lebourg Collection, Gadsden
Frank Lebourg's collection of fine photographs by his father, Albert Lebourg, emphasizes family and recreational activities in the Gadsden area.

Library of Congress, Washington, D.C.
Photographs from the Farm Security Administration and Office of War Information are in the Library of Congress. Hundreds of outstanding photographs of Alabama during the depression and in the war years are included. Photographers for the FSA/OWI who worked in Alabama include Arthur Rothstein, Walker Evans, Dorothea Lange, Marion Post Wolcott, Jack Delano, Ben Shahn, Russell Lee, and John Collier.

Maxwell Air Force Base, Air University Office of History, Montgomery
This collection is especially valuable for pictures of wartime activities in Montgomery and Tuskegee.

H. E. Monroe Collection, Huntsville
This is an extensive collection of prints and negatives that is valuable for pictures of social and economic activity in Madison County for the past century.

Redstone Arsenal, Public Affairs Division, Huntsville
The Arsenal maintains a limited file of photographs documenting the facility's growth and development.

Tennessee Valley Authority, National Fertilizer Development Center, Muscle Shoals
The photographic division has assembled an excellent collection of prints and negatives that tell the story of federal activity in the Muscle Shoals region.

Tuskegee Institute, Washington Collection, Hollis Burke Frissell Library
Outstanding photographs of activities at Tuskegee Institute and of black rural life throughout the period fill this large collection.

The University of Alabama, William Stanley Hoole Special Collections Library, Amelia Gayle Gorgas Library, Tuscaloosa
The Woodward Iron Company Collection of TCI photographs, a variety of Farm Security Administration prints, the Walter B. Jones Collection, and the files of the university's Pictorial History Project are all valuable.

University of South Alabama Photographic Archives, Mobile
The Erik Overbey, the S. Blake McNeely, and the Alabama Dry Dock and Shipbuilding Company collections offer unrivaled coverage of the area's development throughout the period, including the critical years of World War II.

Suggestions for Further Reading

Agee, James, and Walker Evans. *Let Us Now Praise Famous Men.* New York, 1941.

Armbrester, Margaret England. "John Temple Graves and the New Deal, 1933–1940." M.A. thesis, Vanderbilt University, Nashville, 1967.

Atkins, Leah Rawls. *The Valley and the Hills, An Illustrated History of Birmingham and Jefferson County.* Woodland Hills, Calif., 1981.

Bailey, Barbara Connell. "Ten Trying Years: A History of Bessemer, Alabama, 1929–1939." M.A. thesis, Samford University, Birmingham, 1977.

Barnard, William D. *Dixiecrats and Democrats: Alabama Politics 1942–1950.* University, Ala., 1974.

Bond, Horace Mann. *Negro Education in Alabama: A Study in Cotton and Steel.* New York, 1939.

Brown, James Seay, Jr. *Up Before Daylight: Life Histories from the Alabama Writers' Project, 1938–1939.* University, Ala., 1982.

Brownell, Blaine A. "Birmingham, Alabama: New South City in the 1920s." *Journal of Southern History* 38 (February 1972): 21–48.

Brownell, Blaine A., and David R. Goldfield, eds. *The City in Southern History.* Port Washington, N.Y., 1977.

Caldwell, Erskine, and Margaret Bourke White. *You Have Seen Their Faces.* New York, 1937.

Carmer, Carl. *Stars Fell on Alabama.* New York, 1934.

Carter, Dan T. *Scottsboro: A Tragedy of the American South.* New York, 1969.

Cason, Clarence. *90° in the Shade.* Reprint edition, University, Ala., 1984.

Chalmers, David M. *Hooded Americanism: The History of the Ku Klux Klan.* Chicago, 1968.

Dennis, Bobby. "Industrial Growth in Northwest Alabama Since 1933." *Journal of Muscle Shoals History* 7 (1979): 142–50.

Dooling, Dave, and Sharon Dooling. *Huntsville: A Pictorial History.* Virginia Beach, 1980.

Elovitz, Mark H. *A Century of Jewish Life in Dixie: The Birmingham Experience.* University, Ala., 1974.

Evans, Walker. *Walker Evans at Work.* New York, 1982.

Flynt, J. Wayne. *Montgomery, An Illustrated History.* Woodland Hills, Calif., 1980.

———. "Religion in the Urban South: The Divided Mind of Birmingham, 1900–1930." *Alabama Review* 30 (April 1977): 108–34.

Gatlin, Patricia. "Henry Ford and the Muscle Shoals Area." *Journal of Muscle Shoals History* 6 (1978): 101–07.

Goodrich, Jillian. "Romance and Reality: The Birmingham Suffragists, 1892–1920." *Journal of the Birmingham Historical Society* 5 (January 1978): 5–21.

Gray, Daniel Savage. *Alabama: A Place, A People, A Point of View.* Dubuque, 1977.

Hamilton, Virginia Van der Veer. *Alabama: A Bicentennial History.* New York, 1977.

———. *Hugo Black: The Alabama Years.* University, Ala., 1982.

Harris, Carl V. *Political Power in Birmingham, 1870–1921.* Knoxville, 1977.

Hollis, Daniel W., III. *An Alabama Newspaper Tradition: Grover C. Hall and the Hall Family.* University, Ala., 1983.

———. "The Hall Family and Twentieth-Century Journalism in Alabama." *Alabama Review* 32 (April 1979): 119–40.

Holt, Thad. "Establishment of Unemployment Relief Agencies in the Hoover-Roosevelt Era." Manuscript in Alabama Department of Archives and History, Montgomery.

Hubbard, Preston J. *Origins of the TVA, The Muscle Shoals Controversy, 1920–1932.* New York, 1961.

Huntley, Horace. "Iron Ore Miners and Mine Mills in Alabama: 1933–1952." Ph.D. dissertation, University of Pittsburgh, 1977.

Johnson, Evans C. *Oscar W. Underwood: A Political Biography.* Baton Rouge, 1980.

LaMonte, Edward S. "Politics and Welfare in Birmingham: 1900–1975." Ph.D. dissertation, University of Chicago, 1976.

Loftin, Bernadette. "A Social History of the Mid-Gulf South; Panama City to Mobile, 1930–1950." Ph.D. dissertation, University of Southern Mississippi, Hattiesburg, 1971.

McLaurin, Melton, and Michael V. R. Thomason. *Mobile: The Life and Times of a Great Southern City.* Woodland Hills, Calif., 1981.

McMillan, Malcolm C. *Yesterday's Birmingham.* Miami, 1975.

McWilliams, Tennant S. *A New Day Coming: Alabama and the Problem of Change, 1877–1920.* Troy, Ala., 1978.

Newton, Wesley P. "Lindbergh Comes to Birmingham." *Alabama Review* 26 (April 1973): 105–21.

Parker, Sandra. "Wheeler Dam and its Influence." *Journal of Muscle Shoals History* 6 (1978): 108–13.

Rosengarten, Theodore. *All God's Dangers: The Life of Nate Shaw.* New York, 1974.

Rothstein, Arthur. *The Depression Years as Photographed by Arthur Rothstein.* New York, 1978.

Sellers, James B. *The Prohibition Movement in Alabama, 1702–1943.* Chapel Hill, 1943.

Shaw, Richard A. "The United Mine Workers of America and the 1920 Coal Strike in Alabama." *Alabama Review* 28 (April 1975): 104–28.

Sherman, Merle. "Industrial Development and the Growth Patterns of Urban Centers in Northern Alabama." *Journal of Muscle Shoals History* 7 (1979): 103–14.

Snell, William R. "The Ku Klux Klan in Jefferson County, Alabama, 1916–1930." M.A. thesis, Samford University, Birmingham, 1967.

————. "Masked Men in the Magic City: Activities of the Revised Klan in Birmingham, 1916–1940." *Alabama Historical Quarterly* 34 (Fall-Winter 1972): 206–27.

Stryker, Roy Emerson, and Nancy Wood. *In This Proud Land: America 1935–1943 as seen in the FSA Photographs.* Greenwich, Conn., 1973.

Tindall, George Brown. *The Emergence of the New South, 1913–1945.* Baton Rouge, 1967.

Ullman, Edward L. *Mobile: Industrial Seaport and Trade Center.* Chicago, 1943.

Wolfe, Suzanne Rau. *The University of Alabama: A Pictorial History.* University, Ala., 1983.

Works Progress Administration. *Alabama: A Guide to the Deep South.* New York, 1941.

Index of
Photographic Collections

Alabama Department of Archives and History, Montgomery, Alabama:

    Picture Files, Library Division, 22, 26, 27, 29, 37, 40, 41, 59, 77, 79, 98, 101, 113, 126, 162, 164, 190, 261, 270

    Jefferson County Free Library Collection, Manuscripts Division, 38, 69

    Mrs. J. L. (Millie) Prentiss Collection, Manuscripts Division, 282

Anniston–Calhoun County Public Library, Anniston, Alabama:

    Alabama Room, 23, 142, 285, 286, 287

Auburn University Archives, Auburn, Alabama, 72, 73, 116, 186, 187, 253, 256, 257, 269

    Agricultural Experiment Station/Cooperative Extension Service Collection, 51, 57, 60, 119, 121, 122, 124, 125

    Laura Watt Hanson Collection, 24

Bessemer Hall of History Museum, Bessemer, Alabama, 53, 82, 83

Birmingham News, Research Library, Birmingham, Alabama, 114, 115, 145, 221, 223, 224, 225, 228, 232, 233, 280, 292, 293

Birmingham Public Library, Department of Archives and Manuscripts, Birmingham, Alabama, 58, 62, 66, 68, 84, 90, 91, 92, 93, 97, 99, 104, 112, 136, 163, 165, 167, 178, 179, 180, 184, 192, 194, 198, 199, 207, 209, 234, 238, 239, 245, 283

    O. V. Hunt Collection, 19, 25, 28, 36, 52, 54, 55, 94, 100, 111, 128, 133, 200, 202

Jackie Dobbs Collection, Birmingham, Alabama, 140, 193, 220

Florala Public Library, Florala, Alabama, 161

Huntsville–Madison County Public Library, Henry B. Zeitler Room, Huntsville, Alabama, 48, 49, 222, 229, 236, 237

    James Record Collection, 213

Jerry Landrum Collection, Florence, Alabama, 50, 76, 103, 166, 290, 291

Frank Lebourg Collection, Gadsden, Alabama, 42, 44, 45, 47, 78, 88, 89, 129, 182, 203, 204, 205, 208, 240

Library of Congress, Washington, D.C., Farm Security Administration/Office of War Information Collection, 130, 134, 135, 138, 139, 141, 143, 144, 146, 147, 148, 149, 150, 151, 152, 153, 154, 155, 156, 157, 158, 159, 160, 168, 170, 171, 172, 173, 174, 175, 176, 177, 196, 197, 206, 214, 215, 226, 227, 230, 259, 274, 275, 276, 277

Maxwell Air Force Base, Air University Office of History, Montgomery, Alabama, 127, 260, 262, 263

H. E. Monroe Collection, Huntsville, Alabama, 67, 118, 290, 291

Redstone Arsenal, Huntsville, Alabama, 255

Tennessee Valley Authority, National Fertilizer Development Center, Muscle Shoals, Alabama, 32, 33, 34, 102, 244, 254

Tuskegee Institute, Washington Collection, Hollis Burke Frissell Library, Tuskegee, Alabama, 21, 56, 74, 75, 85, 117, 120, 123, 188, 195, 212

The University of Alabama, William Stanley Hoole Special Collections Library, Amelia Gayle Gorgas Library, Tuscaloosa, Alabama, 20, 71, 189, 191, 258

    Woodward Iron Company Collection, 46, 63, 64, 65

    Walter B. Jones Collection, 70

The University of South Alabama Photographic Archives, Mobile, Alabama, 169

    Alabama Dry Dock and Shipbuilding Corporation Collection, 242, 243, 246, 247, 248, 249, 250, 251, 252, 265, 266, 267, 268, 272, 273, 278, 279, 281, 284, 288, 289

S. Blake McNeely Collection, 185, 211, 217, 218, 219, 241

Erik Overbey/Mobile Public Library Collection, 18, 30, 31, 35, 39, 43, 61, 80, 81, 86, 87, 95, 96, 105, 106, 107, 108, 109, 110, 131, 132, 137, 181, 183, 201, 210, 216, 231, 235, 264, 271

About the Author

Michael V. R. Thomason is Professor of History and director of the Photographic Archives at the University of South Alabama. He received his bachelor of arts degree at The University of the South (Sewanee) and his master of arts degree and doctorate from Duke University. He is co-author of *Mobile: American River City; The Image of Progress: Alabama Photographs, 1872–1917;* and *Mobile: The Life and Times of a Great Southern City.*